A Continuous Miracle

Hildegard Dehmel Jensen

an imprint of Imagine! Books™ • Columbus Ohio

A Continuous Miracle
by Hildegard Dehmel Jensen

Copyright © 2004 by Ruth L. Orewiler

All rights reserved. No part of this publication may be reproduced or transmitted in any form or by any means, including informational storage and retrieval systems, without permission in writing from the author or publisher, except for brief quotations in a review.

Edited by Kristen Eckstein
Cover and interior design by Joe Eckstein

Published by Jubilee! Press™, an imprint of Imagine! Books™
part of Imagine! Studios™
P.O. Box 547, Galloway, Ohio 43119
Email: contact@imaginestudiosonline.com
www.imaginestudiosonline.com

Scripture quotations marked (NIV) are taken from the *Holy Bible, New International Version®*. NIV®. Copyright © 1973, 1978, 1984 by International Bible Society. Used by permission of Zondervan. All rights reserved.

Scripture quotations marked (LB) are taken from the Holy Bible, Living Bible Translation. Copyright ©1971. Used by permission of Tyndale House Publishers, Inc., Wheaton, Illinois 60189. All rights reserved.

All other Scripture quotations are from the *Holy Bible, King James Version* (KJV).

ISBN 0-9764353-5-7 (hardback)
ISBN 0-9764353-6-5 (paperback)
(previously 1-932966-01-3)
Library of Congress Control Number: 2005922353

First Jubilee! Press™ hardback and paperback printing: February 2005

Preface

When Dr. Rosmarin entered the conference room of the hospital and gave us the news that Mother was very ill, and — without another miracle — she would not be living in this world much longer, I was devastated. Mother's book was far from finished — in the book she hadn't met my father yet, and what I really wanted her to tell were all those faith-building stories about their pioneer ministry. Well, that was not to happen.

Although Mother's book didn't get finished, I thought I'd look through the files and notes and see if we could utilize what she had written. The following manuscript will contain the seven completed chapters from birth to age eighteen, followed by a few short true stories that took place later in her life, a sermonette, and a few poems she had written. I trust you will find these words educational and inspirational.

Ruth Jensen Orewiler

Dedication

Dedicated with appreciation to my daughter, RUTH JENSEN OREWILER for her support and the fire behind my writing—

and to HELEN C. GRAHAM for her encouragement, inspiration, and assistance in getting this book written.

Also to the MANY FRIENDS who inspired me, prayed for me, and gave me the incentive I so much needed.

Lastly, to my GODLY HERITAGE—MY MOTHER, who prayerfully instilled the seeds of faith into my life. WHAT I AM, I OWE TO MY MOTHER.

Contents

Preface | 3

Dedication | 5

Introduction | 9

Prologue | 11

Chapter 1 | 17

Chapter 2 | 29

Chapter 3 | 45

Chapter 4 | 61

Chapter 5 | 71

Chapter 6 | 81

Chapter 7 | 93

Short Stories | 117

Short Sermon | 147

Poetry | 155

About The Author | 173

Introduction

For a long time, I have been encouraged to write an autobiography of my life. Then I dropped the thought and my mind was never at rest. There were so many Divine interventions in my life and those of my parents' — as well as healings and miracles. I feel obligated to share them and give God the glory.

In St. John 15:27, Jesus, speaking to His disciples, said, "And you also must testify" (NIV). I am now witnessing the things I have seen, heard, and experienced.

In May of 1988, Helen C. Graham, a reporter for the Ontario Tribune-Courier, interviewed me for an article she submitted to the newspaper. When she was finished, she suggested that I write a book and title it *A Continuous Miracle*.

Shortly afterward, my daughter Ruth handed me a package of tapes and said, "Here, Mom, takes these and get started on your book. Your experiences are all in your heart and mind, but, we will never know them if you don't write them down."

In January of 1994, I shared my testimony at a women's Aglow meeting. After that, I received a phone call from Linda Moritz. She asked me if I had started my book yet.

I told her, "No."

Linda then said, "You ought to. Let me help you."

Since this was the third urging, I decided, with God's help, to write my book. I have taken Helen C. Graham's idea and named my story *A Continuous Miracle*.

A CONTINUOUS MIRACLE

Interwoven into the threads of my life are outstanding healings and Divine interventions. I trust these will become an incentive for greater faith in God and His promises.

Prologue

My life is unique. I was saved at the age of five and filled with the Holy Spirit at eight. My mother, Johanna, taught me spiritual values from my childhood. I was sheltered from the gross sins and corruptions of this world. When I was facing a decision, Mother would ask me, "What would Jesus do?" Thus, I made my own decisions and did not feel as though I were being manipulated. I thank God for a good heritage, which, to me, is of greater value than gold.

My mother came from an "elite" family — the Riekehofs of Lage, Lippe, West Germany. They were businessmen, factory and hotel owners, and one was a mayor. My mother's father, Heinrich Riekehof, was the manager of a brickyard in Muelheim. My father's father, Karl Dehmel, purchased his bricks there. The Riekehofs were Godly people and attended the Dutch Reformed Church. However, there, they were never taught the plan of salvation. Mother was very sensitive to spiritual things. From her earliest recollections she was searching for truth.

On her Confirmation Day, Mother asked her pastor, "Does this make me a Christian, and will it ensure heaven?"

He replied, "Oh, yes, Johanna."

"That's strange," she commented, "I don't feel any different now than I did before."

He then replied, "Oh, Johanna, if all the people were as good as you are, they would all go to heaven." Mother was disappointed but kept searching.

When she was eighteen, Mother went to Muelheim a/d Ruhr, to work at a bakery. While there, she met a young lady who led her to the Lord. She became an ardent reader of the Word of God. From the time of her salvation, she had an uncanny faith which she exhibited until the Lord took her home. Shortly before going to Muelheim, she met her husband.

Mother and Father's romance would make an interesting "fairy-tale." Mother was eighteen years old when she first met my father. She was the oldest of a family of four, and was caring for her siblings while her mother was at the hospital in Muelheim attending to a very sick husband.

At that time, it was customary for the military, when maneuvering troops, to stop at the closest city for night lodging. Every family in town was compelled to take one or two soldiers, giving them sleeping accommodations and breakfast, before the soldiers traveled on.

My mother was distressed by this news. She went to the authorities and asked to be excused. She explained to them her situation and told them that since her mother was at the hospital with her sick father, she was alone with her brothers and sister. "It isn't proper for a young girl to be in the house alone with a stranger," she said. "Please, don't put me through this."

However, Lage was a very small town, and there were more soldiers than accommodations for them. The authorities assured her that they would do their best, but she better prepare for soldiers to come.

It was evening, and her neighbors had already received their guests, but she had not. Did this mean that her request had been granted, and that they were not coming? Alas! — just when her hopes were high, she heard the firm footsteps of someone coming down the walk, and saw the tip of the shining helmet. No, she was not

Unteroffizier Wilhelm Dehmel

spared. But instead of two soldiers, there was only one.

Mother went to answer the door, and Unteroffivier Wilhelm Dehmel introduced himself. He was very polite and made a deep impression on my mother. She led him to the table where the meal was waiting in family style. But then, instead of starting a conversation with him, she excused herself, took the siblings outside, and sat on the porch. She was too shy to stay around.

Wilhelm felt forsaken and isolated, but when he was through eating he began searching for the hostess, finding her sitting on the porch with her clan around her.

"May I join you?" He asked as he settled on the steps. My mother, Johanna, felt flushed. This was a new experience, and she felt very uncomfortable. But soon an interesting conversation began. She learned that this soldier's father knew her father. You see, Karl Dehmel, Sr. was a bricklayer and he bought all of his bricks at the brickyard where Mother's father, Heinrich Riekehof, was the manager. That broke the ice, and they both learned a lot about each other.

After William had left the next morning, Johanna spied his canteen on the kitchen table and knew he must have forgotten it. She figured it needed to be returned to him or he would receive a demerit. She knew she couldn't let that happen! In her excitement, she couldn't find her good shoes. So, slipping into a pair of her wooden ones, she grabbed the canteen and took off.

The soldiers were all gathered at the market place. All had now arrived for their orders to come through. What a fine looking group they were. There standing at attention was William, in the center of the first row.

"Clump-i-ty clump, clump-i-ty clump, clump-i-ty clump" was a sound that came closer and closer. Everyone turned to see where it was coming from and what was making that noise. Suddenly Johanna appeared holding the canteen in her hands.

Having reached the soldiers, she looked over the group. Spying William, she excitedly called, "Herr Taube, Herr Taube, you forgot this!"

William was so embarrassed he would have been relieved if the earth would have opened and swallowed him. He snatched the canteen from her hands and stepped back into line to avoid being noticed as much as possible.

That very moment, orders came through. Before anyone could make a comment, the commanding officer's voice could be heard with the new orders. With a sigh of relief, William marched on, while Johanna happily returned home, never realizing what an embarrassing moment this was for the young man she secretly admired.

The next morning as Wilhelm left he asked for Johanna's address and for permission to write her. That started a courtship that ended in marriage performed by Reverend Traub in Muelheim, seven years later, on May 7, 1906. Speaking of her marriage, Mother used to say, "I found my husband in back of the kitchen stove."

My father was a born-again Baptist and came from a family of brick masons. They had twelve children. Six died at an early age and six lived to a ripe old age. They had two sets of twins. There were five boys and one girl.

Wedding Photo, Johanna (Riekehof) and Wilhelm Dehmel, May 7, 1906 in Muelheim a/d Ruhr, Germany

Chapter 1

MY BIRTH

It was a bright sunny day and Johanna was collecting pennies for the building fund for the Baptist church. Walking was unusually strenuous, so she stopped at her friend Rosa's house to rest. Rosa's coffee pot was always hot. She poured Johanna a cup, saying, "Here drink this. You look exceptionally tired today. How many pennies have you collected?"

"Oh," replied Johanna, "I started early and am glad I did. I don't feel as perky as usual and will be glad to get home. I haven't counted the pennies yet but this is the most I've ever collected." As she was speaking, she experienced a sharp pain, which Rosa noticed.

"What's wrong, Johanna?"

"I don't know. I have never had a pain like this before," answered Johanna.

"Are you sure you're not in labor?" asked Rosa.

"Oh, no. I have another week to go," was the reply.

"There is never a set time," explained Rosa. "Babies may come sooner or later than expected. If I were you, I would go straight home. It looks like the real thing to me."

Upon Rosa's advise, Johanna went right home. On the way, she had another sharp pain and stopped between two buildings to double over.

When Johanna got home, she immediately called the midwife. In those days, it was common to have babies at home with the aid of a midwife. When Mrs. Emma Taube arrived, she examined Johanna at once and confirmed that she was, indeed, in labor. However, the birth was not without complications. Johanna had a retained placenta and the physician had to be called. With his expertise and God's help, the problem was soon solved. I was born ten minutes past midnight on September 16, 1909, in Muelheim. Everyone in the family was wishing I had been born on the 15th, for that was my uncle Henry Riekehof's birthday. Later he married Laura Warweg, whose birthday was also on the 16th. We all celebrated together.

THE FIRST MIRACLE

Shortly after my parents were married, Mother found out she was barren. They were both disappointed. My father took Mother to a nearby hospital where they treated only female disorders. She was admitted, and after six months of daily treatment, was discharged as a hopeless case. While she was there, the doctors discovered cancer in her uterus. This did not discourage Mother because her faith in God was strong.

"I don't care what anyone says. I have a big, wonderful God and He is able!" exclaimed Johanna. "I am going to live and bear a child. My name is Johanna, and as Hannah of old was also barren and gave birth to Samuel after praying, so I, too, will have a child." Shortly afterwards, Mother conceived. She went full term and delivered a healthy child. My birth was the first miracle.

Hildegarde Dehmel Jensen

MY NAMING AND DEDICATION

My birth brought great excitement to the family, especially since I was the first grandchild on my mother's side, and they all gathered together to name me. My father was a military man and had served in the army for seven years, intending to make it his career. To please my mother, who was uncomfortable with that idea, he dropped out. He went to work for his brother Karl, an architect and builder, but when it came to naming me, his military expertise surfaced. He chose the name Hildegard, meaning, "battle maid." Mother chose Elizabeth, and my father's mother wanted me named after her—Augusta. My mother's mother wanted the name Louise. Since they could not come to a decision, the naming was tabled. That very day the first zeppelin flew over

Family portrait — Wilhelm Dehmel, Johanna Dehmel, and 3-year-old daughter, Hildegard Dehmel

our house and I was named Zeppelina for the next several days.

A week later they met again and this time they drew straws. My father pulled the longest one, so he got his wish, and I was named Hildegard. Mother's choice was second. In order not to offend anyone, the other names were added. I have four names on my birth certificate: Hildegard Elizabeth Augusta Louise Dehmel. A short time later, I was dedicated, or as some say, christened. It was done at the Baptist church by Reverend Carl Traub. My parents stood together and thanked God for answering their prayer, then my mother rededicated me to His service.

STORMY WEATHER AHEAD

The Dehmel Construction Company was flourishing and Father felt secure working for his brother, Karl. One day he came home in a dejected mood. My mother picked up on it immediately and asked, "What's wrong?"

"Karl is in trouble and I don't know how it will turn out," Father replied. "It doesn't look good. Karl gave an estimate for laying out Elm

1912, Dehmel Construction Company. Wilhelm Dehmel, foreman of this construction crew in Germany, is on the extreme left.

Street and he got the contract. Today he began surveying the job and discovered there is quicksand involved. The entire street will have to be reinforced in order to hold back the ground. This would cost an enormous amount and Karl did not figure it in."

Karl went to the authorities and disclosed his findings. He informed them he could not do the job for the price he quoted. The reply was, "We will hold you to your contract and that is your problem. You work it out." Karl began the job hoping the quality of the ground would change, but it didn't, and soon he ran out of money. The city took possession of all his belongings and they placed a stamp called "kuckuk" on everything including his furniture. "Kuckuk" indicated that someone's belongings had a lien placed on them by the government and that those belongings could not be sold. This was very degrading and took its toll on his wife, Katherine. Class distinction was of great importance in Germany, and to drop from the high class to the lowest was embarrassing and more than Katherine could take. Karl had laid aside a few hundred mark for a rainy day—which came in handy. He also had a close friend, Reinhold Winter, who Karl kept in touch with, even though Reinhold had gone to America. Karl wrote and told Reinhold of his dilemma. "Salvage what you can, come to America, and make a new start. I'll back your affidavit," was Reinhold's reply. So that's what Karl did. He took his wife, Katherine, his son, Karl Jr., and daughter, Katie, and sailed for America in 1911.

Now, this left my father without a job. That night, my parents discussed the happenings of the past few months and Mother quoted Romans 8:28:

"And we know that all things work together for good to them that love God, to them who are the called according to His purpose."

She wondered how this could fit into their lives, but little did she know this was only the beginning of more stormy weather ahead. Their faith was to be tried even further. Would they survive?

Father, a good stonemason, soon found employment with a demolition company that also worked in construction. Things went well, and he found favor with the supervisors. As time passed, he heard from Karl in America. Karl had settled in Elizabeth, New Jersey, which was a thriving city just twenty five miles from New York City, across the Hudson River on the New Jersey side. In that city was an entire German settlement. All of the men worked at the Singer Sewing Machine factory, a large factory where German was spoken as freely as English. Karl felt at home there, but missed his family. So he wrote to his brother, Wilhelm, my father, and asked him to come to America and join him there. He said: "This is a good country and you will have a better chance to get ahead here than in Germany." My father dragged his feet and Mother was also reluctant. She did not want to leave her nice home and her family. Her uncle, Adolph Riekehof, was the owner and operator of a well-known furniture factory. Their furniture had a touch of elegance, and the elite from all over Germany did business with him. When my parents were married, Uncle Adolph furnished the complete apartment with the best chattel. This was difficult for my mother to leave, so the thought of moving was laid aside.

In the meantime, the city of Muelheim was making some improvements and some store buildings had to be taken down in order to make room for the new buildings. The company for which my father worked got the contract. The foreman instructed that all debris be taken to the city dump. Several days later, my father dropped by the dump. He saw some good pieces of metal, some pipes, and other salvageable material. He was very conservative and reasoned that some of these materials could be recycled. He went to his foreman and asked for permission to reclaim some of the materials. His request was granted. After working hours, my father went to the dump and retrieved some of the valuable scrap. He sold it, and to his surprise, discovered it amounted to quite a bit of money. When his foreman saw the value of it, in order to cover up his apathy to recognize its value, he reported my father as a thief. Instead of thoroughly investigating the incident, the company fired him. This was too much for his pride. He was an honest man and to put this kind of accusation against him was more than he could take. This situation changed his mind and he said, "Johanna, I'm going to America. You and Hilde can stay here until I send for you. I'm going on ahead to earn money for your steamship tickets. With Katherine's help, I'll get an apartment and furnish it. When it's ready, I'll send for you."

SACRIFICE AND DIVINE INTERVENTION

It was painful for my mother to leave because, first, her mother was a widow and needed her. They were very close. After my mother's salvation, she led her mother to the Lord and their ties were even closer. Secondly, we lived in a highly respected, secluded part of town called the "poet's section." Her cozy home and lovely furnishings were difficult to part with. Thirdly, Mother enjoyed listening to the services from the First Pentecostal Church in Germany, which was adjacent to their house. She was cautioned to stay away from these "tongues people" because they were considered a cult. However, her bedroom window faced their window and while in bed having me, she received the full benefit of the services. She detected no error—it only whet her appetite for more and this she did not want to lose. It was, indeed, a sacrifice to give up all this. However, the seeds were planted and she was to reap the fruit later in America.

These incidents proved to be a blessing in disguise. I believe it was Divine intervention, for had they not happened, my father would never have left Germany. If he had stayed there, he would have died, for shortly afterwards World War I broke out and only one man returned home from his entire regiment. His mother wrote him later saying, "The authorities came looking for you, but I told them they would have to go to America if they wanted you." I truly believe these problems and leadings were only blessings in disguise!

FAREWELL TO THE GERMAN HOMELAND

The Riekehof's homestead, Lage, Germany. Looking out of the window is Luise and her two sons. In front are neighbors with Johanna and Hilda Dehmel in the center.

The transition for the move was made immediately and my father left for America in 1913. My mother and I went to Lage to live with her mother, Luise Riekehof. My father sent for us in 1914. We left with my father's brother, Henry Dehmel, and my mother's cousin, August Hill. The parting was very painful for my Grandmother Riekehof. I can still remember seeing her with a towel to her eyes as the train passed her house in Lage.

1913, on the boat Prince Frederick Wilhelm, *going from Germany to America. Left to right – Henry Dehmel, Johanna Dehmel, August Hill (a cousin), and Hilde Dehmel, 3½ years old.*

We left from Rotterdam, Holland on a ship called Prince Frederick Wilhelm, and I became very frightened when the gangplank was taken away. I knew I could not get back to land and the fear of that huge body of water started my tears flowing. Excessive puffs of smoke came from the three smoke stacks or chimneys. The ship's whistle blew loudly and slowly as the ship pulled away from the shoreline into the unknown. Mother held me in her arms and with a clear voice she began to sing (translated):

*"Yes, He understands, all His ways are best.
Hear, He calls to you – come to me and rest.*

Leave the unknown future in the Master's hand.
Whether sad or joyful, Jesus understands."

I don't know whether she was singing that to me or to herself, but it calmed both of us. Soon the land drifted from view and for nine days we saw nothing but water, sky, and stars.

THE VOYAGE

The ocean trip was calm, but Mother was seasick the entire time. She had to lie flat on her back in her bunk in our small cabin. There was a small porthole overlooking the ocean and the splashes of water against the window were all Mother saw. Not so with me, for I was all over the ship. The passengers, stewards, and even the captain were attracted to this little, chubby, talking machine. The captain even took me on his command bridge and, putting me on his lap, he allowed me to hold the big wheel of the steamer. This was exciting! I could have anything I wanted, even chocolate—a specialty for the German people. They offered it to me, but I refused it. One of the stewards told my mother, "Your daughter has more common sense than the older ones. We offered her a chocolate bar but she said, 'No thanks. I don't want to spit!'" I had discovered that chocolate was not the best for seasickness. However, over my berth hung a large pocket made of cloth that was filled with fresh cookies daily, which I enjoyed and made good use of. The nine days passed quickly and, as we neared the American shore, the captain gave me a souvenir. It was a long ribbon with the name of our ship, *Prince Frederick Wilhelm*, printed on it.

The steamer slowed its speed and pulled into a temporary dock on Ellis Island where a doctor came on board to check all passengers. No one with serious illnesses was permitted to enter America and even people with cataracts were returned to their homelands. My father's brother, Herman, was an example. He was the only member of the Dehmel family who remained in Germany because of his eye problem. Anyone who might become a public charge was not admitted. How different from today, when even people with AIDS are allowed in. Mother had gotten up, dressed, and, for the first time, stood on deck to enjoy the fresh air. She also was able to have a full view of the Statue of Liberty, given to the United States by France. One of the immigration officers explained the statue's meaning, but I was too young to understand. This immense statue with its torch left a deep impression on Mother, Uncle Henry, and August. It sparked within us hope and enthusiasm for a new life ahead.

Ellis Island was the immigration headquarters, set up on a twenty-nine acre stretch of ground in the New York Bay, surrounded by the Atlantic Ocean. At this point, the ocean forked into two rivers — the East River, flowing to the right or east of New York, and the Hudson River, flowing to the left or west of the city. The Hudson River was the docking place for all passenger ships. It also formed the boundary between the states of New York and New Jersey. The steamship companies had their piers on both sides of the Hudson River.

When the doctor was through with his examinations, the ship proceeded to its pier. Since the North German Lloyd, which owned and operated our ship, had its pier on the New Jersey side — Hoboken — our ship docked there. It was led by the aid of two tugboats that slowly and successfully guided it to its final mooring.

Then, came the moment of excitement... my father was standing at the pier! The gangplank had been lowered, and since all passengers were released alphabetically, we were among the first to depart. My parents embraced each other. Tears of joy flowed, and I clung to Mother's skirt like a vine to a branch. We took a train, and within twenty minutes, arrived in Elizabeth, New Jersey—our new home.

Chapter 2

ELIZABETH, NEW JERSEY—CITY OF DESTINY

Elizabeth, New Jersey was an industrial city. The Singer Sewing Machine Company and the Standard Oil Company of New Jersey were the largest companies in the area when we arrived. Rail and water transportation were accessible since the city faced the Newark Bay—an arm of the Atlantic Ocean.

Elizabeth Port had a large pier where ferryboats connected Staten Island and New York. Commercial and fishing boats docked there daily. My parents and I would often go to the pier, watch the fishing boats come in,

Hildegard Dehmel, 3 ½ years old when she arrived in the United States.

and then buy some of the fresh catch. That was good eating. The pier was also a recreational center. We would often go on Sunday afternoons to enjoy the cool ocean breezes and chat with friends and neighbors.

Division Street, the street on which we lived, divided the city. To the east were Elizabeth Port and the pier. To the west was Broad Street, the shopping center we referred to as "Up-town." Here, also, was the railroad station where the New York Central connected New York City and Chicago and parts West. The trains stopped in Jersey City, and from that point, all passengers were transported via ferry to New York City. It was a busy place, especially in the morning when the offices opened. Passengers would often bump into each other in their mad rush to catch the ferry and get to their offices on time.

Since Elizabeth was an industrial city at the point of immigration, many ethnic groups settled there. They formed their own little cities within the city. The Germans, Polish, and Italians settled like clusters of grapes all over the city.

Wilhelm Dehmel and vacationers with his prized Hupmobile.

Division and Smith Streets, plus Rebecca Place, were the German settlement. Many attended the German Baptist Church that was on the corner of Division Street and Rebecca Place. This became a springboard for a greater spiritual outreach.

NEW HORIZONS

Wilhelmina Simmat, or "Minna" as she was called, was a close friend of Mother's. Minna was very active in the Baptist church. Her heart burned with the Pentecostal fire and she so desired to ignite a spark among those around her. Pentecost was relatively new and misunderstood. Minna had received enlightenment while still in Germany. She attended the "Stein Strasse" (Stone Street) Church where we lived and had received the baptism in the Holy Spirit with a call:

"Go to Elizabeth, New Jersey, for I have many people in that city."

This call burned in her heart while she looked to the Lord for guidance and wisdom to fulfill it.

Minna Simmat started prayer meetings in her home. She shared the truths about the Holy Spirit with those who came to the meetings. Mother was one who opened up to this new teaching. She had received a glimpse of it in Germany and now desired to know more.

In these meetings in Mrs. Simmat's house, some were saved, healed, and filled with the Holy Spirit. Consequently, many attended. Soon the house was too small. Minna then rented the Baptist Church. She contacted Reverend Arnold from Chicago—an evangelist who flowed in the gifts of the Spirit—and started a revival meeting.

THE PLANTING OF THE FIRST
PENTECOSTAL CHURCH IN ELIZABETH

Mother invited our landlord, Ernest Teufel, who lived next door, to these meetings. He was highly educated, but was an anarchist. He was originally Catholic, but lost his faith in Christianity because of weaknesses within the church. He said, "If that is Christianity, I don't want it." So, he went from one extreme to the other and joined the anarchists.

Mother was burdened for this man and claimed his salvation. I called him Uncle Ernest because Mother taught me never to call older people by their first names. She said that showed a lack of respect.

Mr. Teufel liked me. One evening, as he returned from work, I ran to him, greeting him, and said, "I worked very hard today."

He replied, "Then you must be very tired."

"Oh, no! What you do for Jesus doesn't make you tired."

This angered him, and he said, "What nonsense is your mother teaching you? Now I will go to those meetings and show them a thing or two."

Sure enough, in the first service he was there. He stuffed his pockets with rotten eggs, which he was going to use at the right moment. The church filled up and the service started. Reverend Arnold was introduced. He greeted the people, and then suddenly stopped. The Holy Spirit gave him discernment and he made a comment:

"You called me to preach to the unsaved. You need it first. I see the murder of your unborn child. I see thievery. You cheated on the scales and did not give your customers their right weight. I see adultery. You are cheating on your mate. You must repent and do your first works over again."

Ernest forgot all about the rotten eggs. When the altar call was given, he got up and went forward. He shook Reverend Arnold's hand and said, "You are the first pastor that ever told the truth." You see, Ernest knew these people only too well. He knew what Reverend Arnold had said was true. Instead of using the rotten eggs, he knelt at the altar and became the first convert in those meetings.

God used Mr. Teufel in a mighty way. He gathered together a number of his old friends and relatives and brought them to church. Mighty conviction gripped the people and revival was on. However, the Baptist congregation did not approve of this, and they stopped the meetings. Mrs. Simmat then went looking for another place. She rented a storeroom on New Point Road, furnished it, and it became the foundation of our new church. It was exciting to go to the services, for the Holy Spirit moved in every meeting with new revelation of His power.

MY SECOND MIRACLE

To me, the New Birth is a spiritual miracle. My parents were both born-again believers. Their desire was to see that I, too, would know Christ as my personal Savior.

It was Tuesday—ironing day. Mother pulled up a little stool that Father had made for me. As her iron pressed out the wrinkles in the clothes, spiritual wrinkles were being removed from my heart as well. She told me the great stories of the Bible. She made certain to choose those that I, at the age of five, could relate to. One was about Joseph forgiving his brothers when they wronged him. Another was about David's faith when he released the stone in his sling that killed the giant.

As she was speaking to me, the Spirit prompted her to set the ironing aside, take me into the living room and get out our family Bible. As she opened our Bible, on the front page was a picture of the face of Jesus with the crown of thorns on his brow. The blood was trickling down His face. The artist accented Jesus' pain in his eyes. It caught my attention. I asked, "Who is that?"

Portrait of Christ, artist unknown

"That is Jesus," Mother replied.

"Jesus? I thought he was the Son of God in Heaven. Why is He so sad and suffering so?"

"Because of your sin and mine," she replied. She then explained the story of salvation. That was all I could take. I fell to my knees and wept bitterly. Mother then was prompted to return to her ironing and leave me alone with the Lord; however, she timed me.

A fountain of tears had opened and all my wrongdoings came before me. The Holy Spirit convicted me of the slightest mistakes. I left no stone unturned. Then the fountain dried up, and it was replaced with joy. My conversion was thorough. I knew I was forgiven and saved. I ran to my mother, threw my arms around her, and said, "Mama, Jesus forgave me. Will you forgive me too?"

My mother hugged me, and said, "Yes, Honey, I will."

Mother looked at the clock and saw that I had been praying for half an hour. Sometimes we think young children do not understand, but it is amazing what enlightenment the Holy Spirit can bring to a child. This was true in my case. I had, indeed, prayed through. I am not against group prayer, but sometimes it is not thorough enough. A lasting salvation depends on praying long enough until His Spirit can witness to our spirit that we are the children of God — based on Romans 8:16.

WHAT IS SALVATION?

When we were born the first time, we were born into sin. Not necessarily did we sin, but our forefathers did. Therefore, sin and death reigned in our mortal bodies — according to Romans 5:21.

The second birth is a spiritual birth. This is what we call salvation. Jesus spoke about it when he spoke to Nicodemus in John 3:1-16: "Flesh gives birth to flesh — but spirit gives birth to spirit" (NIV). John 3:6 means it is this spiritual birth that makes Heaven available. The natural body dies and goes to the grave, but the spiritual body lives on.

Let's look at another Scripture in Mark's gospel, Chapter 2:22-22 (NIV):

"No one sews a patch of unshrunk cloth on an old garment. If he does, the new piece will pull away from the old, making the tear worse. No one pours new wine into old wineskins. If he does, the wine will burst the skins and they will both be ruined. No, he pours new wine into new wineskins."

You cannot patch up your old life of sin with what some call religion. It doesn't work. You need a complete new spiritual life—a new garment, new wineskins. You need the NEW BIRTH—SALVATION. Only Jesus can give it to you because it was HE who bore our sins on the cross. You must ask for it.

A FOURTH OF JULY MIRACLE

It was the fourth of July. I was six years old. It was a sweltering, hot day and I wore a thin, cool dress. Since my father had a day off, my parents decided to visit my mother's cousin, August, who was in the hospital. It was evening before we returned. As we approached our house my four-year-old friend, Elizabeth, stood at our gate holding a sparkler in her hand. The brilliant sparks that were being emitted fascinated me. Instead of following my mother into the house, I asked her permission to stay outdoors a little longer.

Mother replied, "Yes, you may, providing you stay right here at the gate. I am going to fix a bite to eat and I want you to come in as soon as I call you."

Mother was scarcely in the house when the sparkler fizzled out. With the still hot stem in her hand, Elizabeth touched my dress and it caught fire. She then said, "You are burning."

I looked down and saw the flames shooting up. I screamed, and before my mother could get to me, I was a living torch.

Thank God for a Godly mother who did not panic in a crisis. She knew how to pray, keep a cool head, and act swiftly. Mother flew to my assistance as she was contacting God.

"Lord, you gave her to me, now please spare her life. Perform another miracle and let the flames not touch her. Spare her like you did the three Hebrew children in the Fiery Furnace."

When she reached me, she threw her arms around me and began patting out the flames. With each stroke she said, "Jesus, Jesus, Jesus." Every time she said, "Jesus," the flame went out. Finally, it was extinguished and she took me into the house. Then she saw the miracle. All of my clothes were ashes. Even between my long flowing hair and my body my clothes were ashes, but my hair was not singed nor my body scarred.

That was my third miracle.

FAITH, HEALINGS, MIRACLES — WHAT ARE THEY?

Faith, healings, and miracles are all on the same wavelength. They are spiritually motivated and spiritually discerned. They cannot be understood by the carnal mind.

"But the natural man receiveth not the things of the Spirit of God: for they are foolishness unto him; neither can he know them because they are spiritually discerned." — 1 Corinthians 2:14

The carnal man wants to see before he believes. He wants evidence before faith. The spiritual man believes before he sees. This is why so many of our brilliant, educated men cannot understand faith. To these men, faith is nil. Nothing can be established unless it is proven. Miracles are the proof of FAITH. You must exercise FAITH first before you can get the proof. So what is FAITH?

"Now FAITH is the substance of things hoped for; the evidence of things not seen." — Hebrews 11:1

How could Abraham have a son when he was one hundred years old, and Sarah, his wife, was past the stage of bearing children? God said it, Abraham believed it, and he received it. That was FAITH in action and it produced the MIRACLE. FAITH is holding the answer in your hand without sight.

Let me illustrate the point. How does anyone know that there is coal in the mine? If there is, how do they get it? The geologist has a map that shows him where the coal veins run. He does not see it, but the map points it out. According to the map, he digs.

The believer has a map—the Bible. According to these instructions he exercises his FAITH.

When the men, by use of the elevator, get to the area where the coal is, how do they get it? A pick and a shovel aren't enough for the task. It must be dynamited. To do that, a fuse is used which is connected to the dynamite. This is ignited and, when the fire gets to the point of contact, the dynamite explodes. It loosens the coal that then is brought to the surface and used.

For the believer, FAITH is the fire that runs along the fuse line until it makes contact—you have the evidence, the answer, and the result. Don't let that fire die out.

At Christmas, my grandson, Byron Orewiler, who lives in Arkansas, came to see me. He brought some fireworks with him and we had a display of fireworks in the snow. One of the firecrackers fizzled out. Why? A strong gust of wind blew the fire out and there was no contact and no explosion.

Often in a Christian's life, winds of discouragement and adversity blow out the fire of FAITH. Therefore, there is no contact and no answer. FAITH must make contact to produce the miracle.

In my mother's case, the news that she had cancer of the uterus and was barren did not kill her faith. She believed God, although the odds were against her, and God honored that faith and gave me to her. She received her MIRACLE. Then she continued to believe for her miracle of healing. During the meeting with Reverend

Arnold, she was prayed for and received that healing. She lived to be ninety-five years old. FAITH paid off. It always does.

THE BIG FIRE

Shortly after the Fourth of July incident, I had another frightening experience. We lived directly across from a horse stable where thirty horses were kept. I never paid close attention to them because they had an efficient security guard and, if I came too close, he would chase me away.

Next door to us lived the Fire Chief, Mr. Gus Gurstung. The gong would ring in his house, as well as in the fire station. It was always loud enough for us to hear it too. Mr. Gurstung was a jolly man. He took me to his station and gave me a tour. He showed me the sparkling engines and the process of cleaning them. Every time they were taken out they had to be polished, even if it was a false alarm. He showed me the second floor where the firemen slept. Next to each person's cot was a large circular opening in the floor through which a pole protruded. When a fire was reported, the men would slip into their suits, slide down the pole right into the fire engine below, and off they would go. He also told me that each street had its own number. Division's street number was seventy-two. Seven long blasts and two short blasts from the alarm would signal a fire on Division Street.

It was still dark. The fire whistle woke me up. I counted and the number was seventy-two. I jumped up, ran into my parents' room, and saw the flames from the stable mirrored in the window. The barn went up like a matchbox and not one horse was saved.

I was very frightened because I thought the fire was in our kitchen. We had only one entrance into the house. The fear of not getting out threw me into shock.

From that time on, I became a "sleep-walker". My parents had to watch me closely. One night, my father followed me into the street before he could catch up with me to wake me up. They even placed a pan of cold water at the foot of my bed, hoping I would awaken when my feet hit the water. It did not work.

Several years later, while in Lebanon, New Jersey, I was prayed for and received my healing. I never walked in my sleep again. It was another physical hurdle I overcame, but it affected my nerves until this day.

GLAD TIDINGS TABERNACLE — 33RD STREET, NEW YORK CITY

My experiences of miraculous deliverances cemented the truth of God's Word even more firmly into Mother's and my lives. However, there was one doctrine she could not clearly understand. It was "Tongues." Were they real, or were they concocted in the mind and then verbally released? Minna Simmat tried to explain it, but Mother just couldn't comprehend. It was clear to Mother why it happened after Jesus' ascension, but why now?

First of all, the coming of the Holy Spirit was prophesied. Secondly, the Parthians, Medes, Cretes, Arabians, and other foreigners who had come to Jerusalem for the feast were told in their own tongue all the things that had taken place. The Gospel was given to these foreigners in their native tongues by people who did not know their languages. This proved to them that these things were true. But, why is it necessary today?

Reverend Robert Brown, the pastor of the 33rd Street church in New York City, and his wife Marie, were well loved. Their services were always inspiring. They were conducting some revival meetings. Minna Simmat rounded together some of her flock and took them to the meetings. My mother and I were among them.

As was customary, when the service was over, there was always an altar call for anyone who wanted to come to pray. My mother went forward and I trailed behind. She wanted to know if this baptism of the Holy Spirit was really from God, and if so, she wanted it too.

She prayed, "Lord, if this from You, please let someone who cannot speak German, speak German when he or she receives the baptism."

While she was yet praying, a young girl in front of her was slain in the Spirit and in a clear voice began speaking in German. The German people never address a stranger with the pronoun "you". They always use "thou." What made this message so distinctive was the way this girl used these pronouns. She started:

"WARUM STEHEN SIE MUESSIG?
RUFET DIE SÜNDER HERBEI
SIEHE, ICH KOMME BALT."

(German)

"WHY ART THOU STANDING IDLE?
CALL THE SINNERS TO REPENTANCE.
BEHOLD, I COME QUICKLY."

(translation)

Then she stopped and spoke in another language. There was a French lady praying next to her.
She said, "She is speaking French."
Mother asked, "What is she saying?"

She was saying the same in French as she had said in German. She then started speaking in German again. This time she changed the pronoun.

"WARUM STEHST DU MUESSIG?
RUFET DIE SÜNDER HERBEI
SIEHE, ICH KOMME BALT."

(German)

"WHY ARE YOU STANDING IDLE?
CALL THE SINNERS TO REPENTANCE.
BEHOLD, I COME QUICKLY."

(translation)

Then she stopped and started speaking in French again. It was still the same message.

To assure herself that this girl could not speak German or French, Mother went to Pastor Robert Brown and asked him. He verified that, indeed, she only knew English. This convinced my mother of the reality of tongues and she thanked the Lord for answering her prayer.

As they were leaving the church, Mrs. Simmat and our group were introduced to Sarah Moore, who owned and operated a Missionary Faith Home.

Many missionaries who arrived in New York had the option to go to her farm and rest for a few weeks before traveling on. This was all free. However, anyone working for Sarah also did it as unto the Lord. Their only pay was room and board.

At the same time our group met Jose Kohn and her two sisters, Emma and Martha, who were staying at the farm and helping with the work. They were also German girls, and a friendship developed between them and Mother. Jose approached my mother with a need they had at the home. She said, "Mrs. Moore needs a man to help with the heavy work at the farm, and Wilhelm would be just the right person. You could assist me in the kitchen. There is always so much to do. Pray about it."

Jose's half-sister, Martha Gartner, who was helping in the kitchen, was leaving to accept a job as lady's maid to a millionaire in New York City. This lady belonged to a church called "The Open Door," whose sole purpose and interest centered on "Missions." Through this lady, Emma Kohn, who had a call on her life, left as a missionary to China. This left Jose alone on the farm with all of the work.

Mother talked to my father about it and they took the need to the Lord. A few days later, during their devotions, Father opened his Bible and his eyes fell on 1 Kings 5:6 – "Now therefore, command thou that they hew me cedar trees out of Lebanon."

This hit him like a brick and he asked, "Johanna, do you think the Lord wants us to go? You know that it would be a life of sacrifice since we would have no pay for our work."

Mother replied, "If God is in this, He will provide."

Little by little the urge grew stronger and they felt God was, indeed, leading them in that direction. A few weeks later, a moving van with two stallions stopped at our door and, in a few hours, we were on our way to Lebanon, New Jersey. This move proved to be a real school for all of us.

Chapter 3

LEBANON, NEW JERSEY

Sarah Moore was a unique person. As a child she found a gun buried in the ground. She did not know it was loaded and, while she was playing with it, it went off and shot off her left hand. She went through life with just her left arm and the stub. However, that did not deter her from doing great things. She overcame her handicap and her life became one of strength despite her weakness.

She was converted and filled with the Holy Spirit when just a young woman, and received the Gift of Faith at the same time. Later she entered the ministry and purchased a farm on Mount Olivet in Lebanon, New Jersey. She converted the farmhouse into an inn and part of the barn into a place of worship. In the summertime she conducted daily services in that barn and the results of her ministry soon spread throughout that entire region. It was referred to as a "camp meeting" and people from the cities around came for a week or two to enjoy the fellowship and the rest. It was operated completely on faith. You gave whatever you wished, and if you didn't have money, it was absolutely free.

It is not all gold that glitters, and Mrs. Moore had another side that was difficult to deal with. She ruled with a rod of iron that was onerous for my father, a former military officer, to cope with. She was legalistic and often narrow in Biblical interpretation. She was very demanding and difficult to work for.

My parents had never lived on a farm before and it was hard to adopt this new lifestyle. Father soon got a handle on the farm work and cared for the cattle like a pro. He learned how to milk and also taught me how, although I was only seven. He plowed and planted corn and, in the fall, we all helped to harvest the crop. I can well remember how Rover, the dog, and I would race between the shocks of corn until we were both out of breath.

I also enjoyed the wide-open spaces. The hill behind our house was great for sledding in the wintertime, and in the early spring it was my delight to find the new nests of eggs the chickens were trying to hide. Yes, there was fun intertwined with work, and the knowledge I received was lasting. As I said before, we all had lessons to learn.

MY LESSONS

I had to learn, at an early age, the message of the "serenity prayer":

"God grant me the serenity to accept the things I cannot change, the courage to change the things I can, and the wisdom to know the difference."

I wanted so much to go out and play with the children that came from the city, but I had to stay in and help Mother with kitchen work.

In the winter I had difficulty getting to school. All the roads were gravel. Farms were far apart and little country one-room schoolhouses dotted the countryside. My school was three miles away and I had to walk that distance twice a day. Our neighbors, the Alpaws, had several children and we would walk together. This helped to lessen the toilsome walk. My friend Alice was a lovely girl, but her brother, Lloyd, was a thorn in my side. In the springtime, we would often feast on wild strawberries along the way. In the wintertime, we'd walk the fences because the snow was too deep on the road. Beware — if we would miss the fence — which occasionally happened. The weather was so bad during February in 1918 that we went to school only one day all month.

OVERCOMING DIFFICULTIES

I learned early in life that bitter comes with the sweet, especially on Mrs. Moore's farm. In the summertime when the city people came, there was much work to do. Sometimes Mother and Jose Kohn fed between forty and fifty people. Since there were only the two of them to do all the cooking and baking, I had to help. Tears and sweat would often pour down my face as I watched the other children play and have fun. I was only a child and I thought life was unfair. Then Mother would try to comfort me. She'd say, "Do this for Jesus. This is good training for harder trials ahead. Jesus is getting you ready now so it will be easier later on." But that was hard for a child to understand.

I was always glad when vacations were over and life returned to normal. I well remember the large, wide, white sweet cherry tree, right in back of our house. These cherries were so good, and I enjoyed climbing the tree's branches to help my father pick them for canning.

A LESSON ON SACRIFICE

It was the middle of December 1917, and as was customary, Mother always had a scripture and a prayer before we went to bed. Today, the scripture was Luke 6:38—"Give, and it will be given to you. A good measure, pressed down, shaken together and running over, will be poured into your lap. For with the measure you use, it will be measured to you" (NIV).

"What does this mean?" I asked her.

In order to make it self-explanatory, she asked, "Hilde, what did you do with the box of hardtacks Mrs. Tritchler gave you?"

"I'm saving it for Christmas," I replied.

"Wouldn't it be nice to send it to your cousin Katie as a birthday gift?" she replied. "Her birthday is on Christmas Day."

That was thorny. Candy, to me, was as rare as snow in May. I cherished that box of goodies. I really struggled with the thought. Why? Katie had so much and I so little. I wanted that candy so bad I could taste it. This was a difficult decision, but I finally consented. With Mother's help, I got them ready for mailing, although hidden tears flowed. Strange as it may seem, I soon dismissed this event and felt happy.

Much to my surprise, a few days later, the mailman stopped with a package for me from Ernest Teufel. I hurriedly opened it and inside was a two-pound box of chocolate-covered cherries! Mother, looking at me, said, "Honey, don't you think it paid to make a sacrifice? Instead of a one-pound box of hardtacks, you now have two pounds of much better candy. Now do you understand what Jesus meant when He said, 'Give and it will be given unto you'?"

This was a lesson I never forgot.

Hildegarde Dehmel Jensen

THE BAPTISM OF THE HOLY SPIRIT AND MY CALL

By this time I was eight years old, and through Mother's teaching, I was more mature in spiritual things. My deliverance from the fire and my experience with Jesus at the time of my conversion created a desire deep within me to please the Lord. I had an intense yearning to receive the baptism in the Holy Spirit, according to Acts 2:4. Mother and I both sought it.

It happened during the summer camp meeting. The Sunday morning service had ended. A missionary from China had shared with us an inspiring message and instead of leaving, we all knelt to pray. Suddenly, there came, like a cloudburst of glory, a move of God over all of us. I fell under the anointing. Then I had a vision. I saw a field of ripe wheat swaying in the breeze. It was ready for harvest but there were no harvesters. Then the Spirit took hold of my tongue and I began speaking in a language I did not know. With it came such an ecstasy of love and joy that it was truly unspeakable and full of glory. It was this power I received that gave me strength throughout my entire life to face any storms confronting me. My faith in God increased and remains unshaken still today.

Sarah Moore explained the vision. "The field is the world. The sheaves of wheat are people who are ready for harvest—for salvation. Since there are no harvesters, God is calling you into the ministry to do his work." Mother's dedication of me was now confirmed.

Mother received her baptism in the Holy Spirit a few weeks later and we were bonded more closely together.

A LESSON IN OBEDIENCE AND MY FOURTH MIRACLE

I had helped my father with chores. Milking was done, and as Father left to go to another part of the barn, he gave me instructions. "Throw down some corn stalks for the cows. When you come back down, don't jump. Use the ladder."

However, instead of obeying, I looked down and thought it would take so much longer to use the ladder. It was more fun to jump and besides, Father wouldn't know. He wouldn't see me. As Eve, I was tempted, disobeyed, and jumped. My foot struck the heavy end of the corn stalk. It tipped over and the full weight of my body hit that ankle and pushed the bone out of place. An excruciating pain, a throbbing sensation, hit my foot and I could not move. I sat there for sometime wondering what to do. "Lord, help me," I prayed, but there was no answer.

My conscience was saying, "Why didn't you obey? It's your own fault. Now see how you will get out of it." I tried to step on it but couldn't. I then decided to hop, supporting myself against the side of the barn. Then to my horror, I saw the bull. He was loose in the barnyard. In terror, I called for my father. He came quickly. "What's wrong?" he asked.

"I can't walk," I replied.

"Why?" Father asked, "Did you jump? I told you not to. That's what you get for disobeying." Then he picked me up and carried me into the house.

I wore high shoes that buttoned down the sides. As soon as the shoe was removed, my foot turned. My toes were sideways. My mother came running and examined my foot.

"There are no broken bones, but she pulled her foot out of the socket," Mother said.

"What shall we do now?" Father asked.

We were thirty miles from the nearest doctor. This was before the time of automobiles and we would have to use the horses and the wagon. That would take a very long time and the jolting would be painful. We had no telephone and could make no appointment. What should be done?

Mother got out the big medical book she had received while in treatment in Germany. She thumbed through it and found a picture of a dislocated ankle. There were some guests in the house, so each one participated in the act. I had to lie on the couch. One person held one arm. The other person held the other arm. One person sat on one leg and another sat on the other leg. Mother then gave my father instructions on how to pull the bone into place. He took the foot into his hand and then also reneged.

"What will happen if I don't do it right?" Father asked.

"If you won't do it, I will," Mother replied. My father's German pride would not allow that, so he pulled. I screamed and it was all over. The foot was straight again. If that would have been the end of it, that would have been the end of it, but there was more trouble ahead. My parents forgot some very important instructions. My foot had to remain elevated to allow the swelling to go down. Instead, they permitted it to hang. I used a footstool as a crutch and, placing the knee of my sore leg on it, walking all over the house. Nothing stopped me from what I wanted to do.

One week passed, a second week passed, and still there was no change. In fact, it swelled even more. Mother then got the medical book out and read it more thoroughly. It said, "Bones can heal, but a stretched ligament never will. It is like elastic. When it loses its elasticity, it is good for nothing but to throw away. Therefore, elevate the foot to reduce the swelling."

She then realized what she had overlooked. Then I had to sit down and keep my foot elevated, but it was too late. The damage was done.

"Our only child and a cripple," Father said. "Oh, no, Lord. Please, no!"

Then Mother's faith jumped into action. She had everyone in the house pray for a miracle. She believed God could do what no man could do, and God would undo her foolish deed of ignorance.

Her faith was now being tested.

The following days brought no change. Another Friday rolled by and I was the same. This time Mother prayed more earnestly. She brought heaven down and everyone felt it. She made contact and shouted, "I have the answer. She will be all right."

That was Saturday, and during the night, God gave me a dream. My father was taking me upstairs to bed. At the head of the stairs was a large glass door. It was dark, and as we approached it, suddenly the door lit up as if a thousand watt bulb were turned on. At that time we had no electricity—we used kerosene lamps. As I studied the source of that light, suddenly an angel appeared in all of his beauty. I dropped to my knees in awe. The angel came over to me, placed his hands on my head, and prayed for me.

This was all it took for my FAITH to jump into action. I woke on Sunday morning and scurried to get out of bed. Mother grabbed me and asked, "Where do you think you are going?"

"I can walk! I can walk! Just let me show you," I replied.

"How do you know? Tell me what happened," Mother demanded.

I told her of my dream. She released her grip, letting me go, and said, "Show me."

I ran down the steps, up the steps, back down again, and all around the house perfectly whole. We had glory in our house that day. Three days later, Mother examined my foot and there was no swelling or discoloration left. "Which foot was it?" she asked. To this day, I have had no trouble with it.

WATER BAPTISM

Hilde Dehmel being baptized in water. September 4, 1917.

I was now nine years old and had not been baptized in water. Mother wanted to make sure that I understood the step I was taking. She then said to my father, "If the Holy Spirit did not deny her the baptism in the Spirit, then we cannot deny her water baptism either." I was then baptized in a creek close to the farm.

This was one of my first experiences of persecution. Lloyd Alpaw, our neighbor, the thorn in my flesh, made sport of my FAITH at school. He embarrassed me in front of my schoolmates. He shouted, "Hilde, I saw you in the creek. What where you doing—catching fish?" Then he laughed and the others joined him.

I had to learn early in life that doing things God's way often caused misunderstanding and distress. It wasn't easy on the flesh but brought joy to the spirit.

LESSONS MOTHER LEARNED — TRIM THE LAMPS

It was my mother's chore to keep the kerosene lamps filled, the wicks trimmed, and the chimneys clean and sparkling. As she was carefully polishing one lamp, the Lord spoke to her soul, "Is the lamp of your life brightly shining, or is the chimney clouded with smoke from a crusted wick? Has your vessel been refilled with oil?"

The past week had been rough. She had worked so hard and it wasn't appreciated. She had been chided for things she had no part in, and her spirit, indeed, was clouded over. Yes, her wick was crusted. She felt pangs of bitterness and resentment forming. Looking heavenward she asked for grace to trim—to cut the memory of the abuse and bitterness from her life. "Refill me with the oil from Heaven and keep my light shining for You." Instantly she felt the crust being removed and a new surge of power rekindled the light in her lamp.

A DESIRE GRANTED

It was a hot Sunday in July 1917 and Mother was exhausted. She had just finished cleaning the kitchen, and with sweat running down her face, she dropped into a chair. She thought, "Wouldn't it be nice to have some cold refreshing ice cream? But that would be like asking for pennies from heaven." She had just finished thinking when the Filhouers arrived for the Sunday afternoon service.

Jose greeted them and remarked, "Why, you are an hour early today."

Grace replied, "Yes, I know, but I thought you might enjoy some of this," and she pulled a container of homemade ice cream out of a box.

Mother shouted, "Glory!" She continued, "Thank you, Jesus. You are so good to fulfill my heart's desire." Then she threw her arms around Grace Filhauer and thanked her. "Isn't it marvelous!" She exclaimed. "The Lord is even concerned about the temporal things of our lives."

NEW STOCKINGS

The day had been unusually busy and Mother found no time to do some of her personal laundry. However, she rinsed out a pair of stockings and hung them out to dry. Later, when she went out to get them, they were gone. What would she do? She had only this one pair. With a deep sigh and a prayer, she returned to the house. "Lord, you know my plight. Please help me. I'm at 'Wit's End Corner' and only you can fix it for me."

It was time for the evening service and Mother said to Jose, "I'll just have to go without stockings. Hope no one will notice it."

"Oh, Johanna, you are too sensitive. No one will look at your legs." Jose had scarcely finished speaking when one of the guests came into the kitchen.

She went straight to Mother and said, "Mrs. Dehmel, I hope you won't be offended, but the Lord urges me to do this. I must give these to you." She handed her two pairs of new stockings.

Thanking her, Mother told her what had happened and said, "You are God's messenger to supply my need." Then they both rejoiced together.

MY DAD

My father was a perfectionist. If Mother had not been such a neat housekeeper, she would have been in trouble. Once, my father ran his finger over the top of the door to see if dust had collected. Even in his personal appearance, he looked stylish and attractive. There was never anything out of place. I was so proud of him.

He was a real father, a home-loving man. He enjoyed classical music. He was kind, gentle, and fatherly. He participated in my school activities and I loved it. He took me on horticulture trips and taught me to enjoy flowers and nature in general.

He took me to Sunday School and introduced the "Cross & Crown System" to encourage faithfulness in attendance. Every year, each person with perfect attendance was given a pin. The first year it was a golden pin with a cross. The second year a crown was added, and every year thereafter a bar was attached. My father had accumulated four bars and then the Sunday School discontinued the system. It was getting too expensive. However, he continued to wear this distinguished pin on his lapel.

When I was seven, before we went to Lebanon, my father converted the basement into a workshop and made Christmas toys for me. It was a kitchen cabinet, a doll bed, and a few doll chairs. He placed them all under the Christmas tree and called it "Hilde's Puppen Stube." Translated this means "doll house."

I was very privileged, for both of my parents gave me all the love and attention I needed. Now that we were in Lebanon, all these things were denied my father. He could only do what Sarah Moore allowed.

Hildegarde Dehmel Jensen

1914, Hilde Dehmel's "Puppen Stube" (Doll House) bed and kitchen cabinet made by her father William Dehmel.

LESSONS MY FATHER ENDURED

My father's first lesson was submission. Capitulating to a woman was a bitter pill for a German military man. To turn over total control to Sarah Moore was difficult for a man's pride.

Another lesson hard to take was lack of privacy. There was no place he could call his own, not even his bedroom. A good example was Christmas 1917. Dad had no money to buy a little something for either Mother or me. In order to brighten up the occasion somewhat, he went into the woods, cut down an evergreen and put it up in our bedroom. Mother and I made paper chains to decorate it. Then we sang carols and I was happy. Suddenly, the door opened and Sarah walked in. When she saw the tree, she went into a rage. "I will have no idol in my house," she screamed.

She went to the window, opened it, and picking up the tree, threw it out. "I hope this will teach you a lesson!" she shouted. With that she left, leaving a broken-hearted little girl, an angry father, and a grief-stricken mother behind. We then formed a circle and asked God to help us overcome all bitterness and again fill our hearts with joy.

Sarah Moore was very domineering, to say the least. She only thought about herself and never took into consideration the feelings of others. One very cold winter day, Father decided to drive me to school.

He said to my mother, "Hilde has lost so much school and it is simply too cold to let her walk three miles. I think I'll get the horses out and take her." I was thrilled. I liked school and missed it when I couldn't go. Just as I was getting into the wagon, Sarah showed up.

She looked at my dad and asked, "What do you think you are doing?"

"Taking Hilde to school," he replied.

"You will do nothing of the kind," she retorted. "My horse Nellie is more important than your Hilde. Nellie is going to be in the battle of Armageddon and I have to take good care of her. Put Nellie back in the stable."

Without comment Father did so, but he swallowed hard to keep from verbal retaliation. Talking to Mother that night, he said, "Johanna, I wonder how much longer I can take this? It's getting more difficult every day."

For a few weeks it was more bearable and then came the straw that broke the camel's back. Father was on his way to feed the pigs when Sarah met him in the barnyard.

"I just read in the paper about the Germans' atrocities"—we were in World War I at the time. "You Germans are all germs who need to be destroyed. I think

I will turn you in as a German spy," she haughtily exclaimed.

My father got so angry he almost poured the bucket of slop over her head. However, he controlled himself and finished the chores. He realized it was a quagmire from which he could not extricate himself, and in order to prevent himself from doing something that he would later regret, he packed his belongings and left. He went to his brother Karl, in Elizabeth, and got a job as a brick mason. Mother and I stayed at the farm until he came and picked us up.

How sad, speaking of Sarah Moore, that a person with God's call on her life could err, fall, lose her anointing, and then end up in confusion.

It would be wise for everyone to heed the instructions given by Jesus in Matthew 7:22, "Many will say to me in that day, Lord, Lord, have we not prophesied in thy name? And in thy name cast out devils? And in thy name done many wonderful works?

And then will I profess unto them I never knew you: depart from me, ye that work iniquity."

Chapter 4

THE AFTERMATH OF WORLD WAR I

Mother was beaming radiantly, holding a letter from my father in her hand. It contained good news.

World War I was over, the Armistice had been signed, and Father had rented a small apartment over a coffee store and was coming to get us. I helped Mother pack and a few days later, we were again on our way to live in Elizabeth.

I liked our new home. Mr. Gus Leisentritt, our landlord and operator of the coffee store, was a friendly and jolly man. He ground his own coffee and had a large clientele because his coffee was always fresh. He also ground peanuts and then sold the peanut butter. It always made my day when Mother would say, "Go down and get a pint of peanut butter." It was so moist and so good, and I would watch it come from the machine. That was fun.

I also enjoyed the school. It was just around the corner and I did not have to take those long walks and miss any more classes. I now had many playmates. We would play "Hide-Go-Seek" or "Red Light—Green Light," as we called it. I got so excited and Mother would ask, "Why are you so loud? I can hear you above all others."

1922, Hilda Dehmel, 8th Grade Graduation

I guess God gave me a loud voice because He knew that I would need it in the future.

AN UNFORGETTABLE EXPERIENCE

It had snowed and snowed as if there were no end. Mountains of snow had piled up like a towering wall. That day, as I was walking home from school, I was enjoying every bit of it. The sun was shining brightly. It had warmed up and I gleefully enjoyed frolicking in the flaky snow. However, I was not aware of what the glare was doing to my eyes. As I opened the kitchen door, everything suddenly turned dark. I could not see and without warning, I suffered the most excruciating pains that I had ever felt. My head and my eyes felt as though they would tear from my shoulders. I rolled on the floor with pain. I could not see. I was snow-blind.

Mother was not at home and I wondered what I should do. When would this end? Would I ever see again? A great fear gripped me. Just then Mother returned and found her hurting, bewildered little girl seeking help.

After questioning me, she realized what had happened. She placed her gentle hands around me, lifting me up, and with a prayer, took me in her arms. She covered my eyes to protect them from further light and prayed for Divine assistance, for removal of all pain, and for restoration of sight. Fear left and I felt snug and secure with her caress.

Little by little the pain lessened and the eyesight returned. But, to this day, my eyes are extremely sensitive to bright light.

ANOTHER MOVE

The apartment over the coffee shop was too small and uncomfortable. Father rented another place on Marshall Street. It was still within the same school district and would not disrupt my studies.

It was a second-story flat, with two granite laundry tubs against the outside wall of the kitchen and a pulley clothesline attached to the kitchen window and to a pole in the back yard. All of the houses were set up in like fashion and it was very colorful, on washdays, to see the clothes swaying in the breeze.

The family living on the first floor were German-Hungarians. They were lovely people, and Mother and Rose Loder were soon knit together as Mary and Martha. Her children and I also became the best of friends. Louise, the oldest, had a learning disability and I spent hours tutoring her. As a "thank you," Mrs. Loder treated me with the best homemade cake with finger-licking chocolate icing. I can still taste it.

The Loders were religious people but they had never been taught about salvation, nor were they introduced to Jesus Christ as personal Savior. This was Mother's opportunity. Gradually, skillfully, she witnessed to them and it paid off. During a series of revival meetings at our church, Rose Loder accepted Christ as her personal savior. She found the missing ingredient in her life and went home rejoicing.

Mr. Anton Loder was a quiet, inward man who never publicly expressed his feelings. He never hindered his family from attending church, although he himself did not go regularly.

Hildegarde Dehmel Jensen

CHURCH GROWTH

The mission on New Point Road bulged at its seams and a new place of worship had to be rented. A much larger storeroom was found on Elizabeth Avenue and the mission moved there.

Carl C. Loenser, who came with the Simmats from Germany, enrolled in Bethel Bible School in Newark, New Jersey. Since the school was very close to our church, he came on weekends and preached for us. During the week, Minna Simmat took charge of the services.

Mother was so thankful that the Loders came into the light that she wanted to do something special for the Lord. She then asked if she could clean the church, without pay, and it was granted. We lived close by, so that created no problem.

From that week, until we moved into our new church building on East Jersey Street, Mother became the custodian. Of course, that included me. Every Saturday that became our chore. I did not mind it too much in the summertime but dreaded it in the winter months. The only heating was a potbelly stove, in which Father would build a fire every Sunday morning. But there was no heat on Saturdays and sometimes it was very cold. My fingers would get stiff, but that was no excuse. I had to go along. God was good and protected us. We never did get sick.

Our group grew by leaps and bounds. There was an influx of German-speaking immigrants who came over after the war. Due to a language barrier, they came to our meetings because they were conducted in German. Besides, many signs and wonders were realized and that brought even more people.

A CONTINUOUS MIRACLE

A MIGHTY MIRACLE

Mrs. Mary Titlus stands out in my mind as one of the greatest women of faith that I have ever met. She had a child-like faith. Besides my mother, she took God at His word and acted upon it. Her children attended church with her but her husband, Joseph, was somewhat reluctant and critical. That did not discourage her and she kept praying for him.

One night, at about three in the morning, he roused her out of sleep and said, "Get up and pray for me. I am going to die today. I'm not saved and I don't want to go to Hell."

She replied, "Oh, Joseph, you had a nightmare, go back to sleep."

"No, I didn't. Please, please pray with me."

"All right." She got out of bed and said to him, "Kneel here beside me." This he did. He then prayed earnestly and asked for forgiveness, weeping his way through until he felt the peace of God in his soul. He then said, "Now I can go back to sleep. Should I die, I know I'm ready."

In the morning they got up as usual. Mary packed Joseph's lunch and they had prayer together before he left.

It was noon. Mary was ironing when the door opened and in walked a black man. It frightened her. Who could this man be and why did he not knock? Then she heard her name. "Mary, don't be afraid. I'm Joseph."

"Joseph, what happened?" Grabbing for a chair, he sat down and unfolded the following incident.

Every noon about five or six of the employees at the Standard Oil Company of New Jersey, where Joseph worked, ate lunch together. One made coffee that they all shared. Today, a new employee made the coffee.

There were three spigots of water side by side. One was cold water, one was hot, and the other was chemical. Not familiar with the spigots, this new man used the chemical faucet, and all who drank were poisoned. All were rushed to the hospital, but Joseph would not go. He said, "Take me home. My wife will pray for me. I have more faith in her prayers than the help the hospital can give."

"Now here I am. Pray for me."

She immediately stormed heaven and prayed fervently. God answered the prayer. His color returned, his pain ceased, and he was made completely whole by the power of God.

This was only one of the many miracles witnessed in that church.

AN UNBELIEVABLE EVENT

An important lesson was taught to me. Satan hinders God's blessings, and we must exercise authority against Satan. Let me illustrate:

The evening service had come to a close. Many went home but some stayed to pray at the altar. Among them was Joe Beda's father. He wanted to be filled with the Holy Spirit and Mother and I went to pray with him. We prayed for quite some time but were getting nowhere. It seemed as if our prayers were hitting a wall and bouncing back.

Pastor Loenser looked at his watch. It was nearing the midnight hour and he wanted to lock up. He then went to Brother Beda and said, "Brother, it is getting late. Don't you think it advisable to stop for tonight? Perhaps, next time, you will receive.

Just then, the Lord opened my mother's spiritual eyes and she saw an imp sitting on Pastor Loenser's shoulder whispering into his ear.

Over the platform was a small window that was open for ventilation.

As Mother saw the imp, she rebuked him in the name of Jesus, and as he vanished through this window, he turned around and stuck his tongue out at my mother and then disappeared. Instantaneously, the atmosphere cleared, the power of God came down, and our brother was filled with the Holy Spirit.

Sometimes Satan binds our prayers, even in a church service, and Satan must be bound and rebuked so that we may become recipients of that which we are asking for — see Daniel 10:12-13.

CARE PACKAGES

In the middle of these miracles, we also experienced the results and ravages of war. Many of our friends received word from their loved ones over-seas asking for help. Our family was no exception.

Grandmother Riekehof wrote expressing her concern over the economy and food shortages. She wrote, "Oh, for a cup of coffee," but there was none to be had. This was in 1919. Shortening, sugar, soap, and other bare necessities used in daily living were not available, Insulin, a medicine that was badly needed, was not available either.

The newspaper then advertised "Care Packages" for $15.00. Essential foods could be sent through this service. My parents availed themselves of this service. However, there was some sustenance not provided through "CARE." My folks then sent packages directly to Germany. They were sent to both sides of the family, the Riekehofs and Dehmels.

The only transportation was by boat and it often took thirty days for packages to get there. Consequently, strict government regulations were enforced. Every package had to be wrapped in cloth and sewed shut. My parents then bought a canning machine, and from that time on, everything was sent in sealed tin cans. Because they were airtight, all of the food was preserved.

That was always a time of excitement for me. Of course, I had to help. In my spirit I could see Grandmother's happy face as she opened her prize package and enjoyed her cup of coffee.

WHY, GOD?

It was noon and Mother had just finished preparing the "Care Package" for mailing. As she was walking toward the door, she heard a voice say, "NO."

"Oh, that must be my imagination. That can't be the Lord," she thought. She continued to the door and as she placed her hand on the knob, she felt an invisible slap on her hand. She turned but saw no one.

"I don't understand. Was that you, Lord?" she asked. Obediently, she placed the package on the table again. A few days later she heard a voice say, "Now go mail your package." Immediately, she took it to the post office, still pondering the delay in her mind. That night she had her answer. Picking up the newspaper, she read:

"The freighter bound for Europe from New York hit a mine and sank." Had she mailed the package when she was restrained from doing so, it would have sunk with the boat. Again she was taught another lesson—it pays to be obedient to the Lord, even if she could not understand.

NEW PLANS

Father had heard that some new skyscrapers were being built in New York City and contractors were looking for brick masons. Since it was dangerous working from scaffolds at such heights, the pay was extra good. It aroused his interest. He applied for the work and was hired.

With this extra pay, my parents were able to lay some money aside to purchase a steamship ticket for Grandmother Riekehof, who had expressed the desire to visit us in America. Arrangements were completed and we were anxiously awaiting her arrival.

THE REUNION

Grandmother Riekehof was arriving. Our local newspaper listed daily boat arrivals, and from that, Father learned that the steamer would be docking at 10:30 A.M. We, that is, Father, Mother, and I, went to meet her. We took the train to Hoboken and walked from there to the pier.

The boat had not yet docked but a crowd had gathered at the gate. We pressed in among the crowd and spotted Grandmother on the boat with the other passengers looking for their families. The boat crew was working with the large ropes to secure the boat as it came into dock. Grandmother spotted us as we saw her. We were so excited she had come, she was here safe in America. It was so good to see her again.

Chapter 5

THE RIEKEHOFS

Grandmother Riekehof was a petite loving woman with many friends. There was never a hair out of place or a spot on her clothes. She had a touch of elegance that drew almost everyone to her. Her hands were never idle. She was always knitting, sewing on buttons, or fixing something. I was proud to call her my "OMA."

Every two weeks she would donate one day to Mrs. Carl

Luise Karoline Kesperling Riekehof, known as Grandma Riekehof.

Spader, who had nine boys. Grandmother would mend socks, patch trousers, and do whatever was needed to keep those husky boys looking trim. Mrs. Spader referred to them as "My Ball Team."

The Riekehofs' Siblings: Helene (died at age 12 with diphtheria), Johanna, Henry, and Paul.

Grandmother had five children of her own. Augusta died in infancy; Helene died at age twelve with diphtheria; and Johanna, Henry, and Paul were still alive. Her husband, my grandfather, had died when I was three years old, and she was free to do as she pleased.

Her youngest son, Paul, was a bachelor and was living with his brother Henry and his wife, Laura. They lived in Lage, Germany and had two girls, Lottie and Ruth.

Paul was a model young man respected by everyone, but he had never made a commitment to the Lord. All his good deeds, his regular church attendance, and godly respect meant little without a personal relationship with the Lord. His mother talked to him about it, my mother witnessed to him by mail, but he remained aloof. All they could do was pray.

Uncle Paul had gone through World War I. As though by Divine protection, he was spared from death when

The Riekehof Family. Seated: Heinrich and Luise; Standing: Henry, Paul, and Johanna

the foxhole in which he was seeking refuge collapsed from an exploding bomb. He was practically buried alive but miraculously lived. He frequently complained about severe headaches, but they did not seem to be a serious threat. However, Grandmother was concerned about him when she left for America.

Months had passed since she arrived. News from Germany was good and she had adjusted and seemed happy and content. I shared my bedroom with her and we adjusted well. I went to her often for advice and she always came through for me.

SAD NEWS

It was Saturday afternoon and we had just finished cleaning the mission. Suddenly, Mother grabbed me and said, "Hilda, pray with me for Uncle Paul. I sense in my spirit that something is wrong. Should he be sick and die, I fear he is not ready. Your uncle possesses an enthusiasm for God, but it is an unenlightened one. He is ignorant of the righteousness provided by God and seeks to establish his own righteousness. That will never do."

We prayed together for some time. Then she said, "I must now hurry home and write him right away. I must, once more, direct him to the true way of salvation."

Several weeks later, after returning from a visit, Mother found Grandmother sitting in a chair weeping bitterly. In her hand she held a letter with a black edge around it. It contained the news that Paul had died. She then gave the letter to Mother to read.

It read: "My dear friends in America—I am the deaconess that took care of Paul, and I have both joyful, as well as, sad news for you. Paul suffered a brain stroke. His brother Henry found him on the kitchen floor unconscious when he went to get a bottle for Ruth in the early hours of the morning. He was rushed to the hospital. His right side was paralyzed and his speech affected. He was very restless for several days. I prayed with him but he wouldn't respond. He seemed to be wrestling with trepidation so I asked him, 'Paul, are you afraid? Jesus died for your sins. Acknowledge Him as your Savior. Ask His forgiveness.' However, there seemed to be no change.

The following day Johanna's letter came. I read it to him and his eyes filled with tears. He reached for the letter with his left hand and drew it to his chest. A smile came over his face and he suddenly changed. His restlessness disappeared and he was quiet and content. He then dozed off into a peaceful sleep.

The following day was Easter. The morning sun shone through the window and he gave me a smile. However, his vital signs were failing and I knew he would not be with us for long. I prayed, 'Dear Lord, give me a sign that he accepted you. I want a definite manifestation that he is born again so that I will have something concrete to pass on to his mother and sister.'

As I stood looking into his apparent lifeless face, he suddenly lifted his paralyzed hand toward Heaven and said in clear tones, "Jesus, Savior." His hand dropped and he was gone. Gone to be with Jesus in that better land.

May these words be a comfort to you.

Signed — Maria"

The death of my uncle Paul cut Grandmother Riekehof to the bone. She was like a bruised reed and could not be comforted. In compliance with her wishes, my father purchased a steamship ticket and she returned to Germany to weep at his grave.

However, she had become accustomed to the "American Way of Life" and no longer felt comfortable in her home. She then wrote expressing her desire to return.

In the meantime, she persuaded her son Henry and his wife, Laura, to go back to America with her. She said, "We will then all be together as a happy family." An agreement was then made that she and Henry would come on ahead and as soon as Henry found a job and got a home ready, his family would follow.

It was a happy day when we went to Hoboken to pick them up. Tears of joy flowed when I hugged my grandmother. She was so precious to me. Uncle Henry was a neat looking man. He had been in the Navy during the war and he carried himself well. His warm congenial disposition pleased me and I knew we would knit well.

Uncle Henry had no trouble finding a job. He was employed by the Singer Sewing Machine Company where he worked until his retirement. At church, Mother introduced him to her many friends and he blended in amazingly well.

PLEASANT CHANGES

The completion of the Ebenezer, an all-speaking German church, brought changes. Pastor Loenser and his wife moved out of our upstairs apartment into the new parsonage. That left a vacancy.

As by Divine providence, Tante (Aunt) Laura and her two girls were on a boat en route to our "blessed country." My mother saw the "hand of the Lord" in this

Uncle Henry's family when they first came from Germany. Left to right: Uncle Henry, Lottie, Ruth, and Aunt Laura.

and she said to my father, "This move just dove-tails with Henry's family coming over. Why don't we fix the apartment up for them?"

"That's good thinking," Father replied, and together with Henry, they immediately took steps to do so. Mother made their needs known to her friends at church, and within a week's time, articles started coming in. Missing items were purchased and, with Mother's professionalism and stunning skill, the living quarters were completed. A bouquet of flowers on the table and a touch of green here and there made it attractive.

I'll never forget that day in 1923 when we went to pick them up. It was a beautiful day and the joy for Uncle Henry was great. I was so proud to hold the charming three-year-old Lottie's hand. Her one-year-old sister, Ruth, was in her mother's arms.

God leads in so many mysterious ways, His wonders to perform. So it was with Lottie. She was destined, in later years after receiving her doctorate, to open a brand-new field of learning for those who wanted to communicate with the deaf. She became the author of the well-known text book "The Joy Of Signing," as well as two others," The American Sign Language" and "Talk To The Deaf."

After arriving home and enjoying a "Welcome" meal, Tante Laura said to her husband, "Take me home. I want to see where I will live."

Mother interjected, "First, let us go upstairs and see Pastor Loenser and his wife." Disappointed, Tante Laura agreed and followed the others, who had already started their ascent.

No one was home, so Mother took Tante Laura through the apartment and asked her, "How do you like it?"

"This is nice", she replied, "but show me mine."

"This is yours", Uncle Henry said. Looking flabbergasted, she responded, "MINE?!" She threw her arms around her husband and wept for joy. We spent many happy years together until they moved to Reid Street, into a house they had bought.

While living in our house on Division Street, two sons were born to them, Henry, Jr. in 1924 and Paul in 1927. They were the first United States citizens in their family.

THE FIRST CHRISTMAS

It was the day before Christmas. The sun was glistening on the snow. The branches of the trees were hanging their heads with nature's crystals, and inside the aroma of pine needles, candles, and freshly baked cookies filled the air.

The door to the living room was sealed tightly and no one was permitted in. The girls were told that room was the Santa Claus workshop. Germans always celebrate their Christmas on Christmas Eve.

Tension filled the air. Ruth was still too young to appreciate it, but Lottie's face was flushed with excitement. Every once in a while, she would peek through the keyhole. The sun had disappeared from the horizon and the tingling of a bell could be heard behind that sealed door. Then, Tante Laura took hold of her girls' hands and said, "It is now time to go in." When the door opened, before their eyes stood a large decorated tree with lights and tinsel, and underneath the tree was a spread of gifts for everyone. There was a big doll sitting in a chair and another one in a doll carriage beside plates filled with candies and cookies. When Lottie saw this, she turned pale. "Honey, this is for you and your sister to play with. No one will take it from you. It's yours." By this time, she had caught her breath, grabbed the doll, and began dancing around the room with it. Everyone enjoyed his or her gifts, and before the night was over, we all sang Christmas carols and gave Jesus his rightful place by thanking him for making it possible.

TESTED

Shortly after moving into their house on Reid Street, my uncle and his family went through a severe test. Henry, a teenager at the time, became seriously ill. It was discovered that he had a brain tumor. He was taken to a hospital in New York. However, little hope was given for his recovery because of the location where the tumor had developed. The entire church prayed for him. My mother encouraged her brother to stand on the word of God. She recalled her past miracles and said, "God will do it again". And He did. The only disadvantage was a limp that Henry mastered beautifully. God had intervened and gave us a miracle.

The Riekehofs' joined the Ebenezer church which, in later years, was renamed Evangel and changed to the English language. Because of growth, they also had to relocate and were now worshiping in Scotch Plains, just outside of Elizabeth, New Jersey.

Uncle Henry and the girls became very active. Lottie and Ruth were both musically gifted. After graduating from high school, Lottie moved away to follow her career. She was Dean of Women for several years at Central Bible College in Springfield, Missouri and then took on a position at Gallaudet University in Washington, D.C. It is the only college for the deaf in the world. In between times, she studied and earned a Doctor's Degree.

Lottie played the piano for my daughter Ruth's wedding. She was also the Maid of Honor in Vancouver, B.C.

Uncle Henry Family Photo: Aunt Laura and Uncle Henry, seated. Standing left to right: Ruth, Paul, Lottie, and Henry.

for my daughter Dolores' wedding. She is presently organist at the Arlington Assembly of God in Virginia.

Ruth has led the Bell choir at Evangel. She has taught Sunday School there and played the organ at Evangel for the church services. She is still doing so today.

Uncle Henry became the Sunday School secretary. He was so efficient that he held that position until death. He was loved and esteemed by everyone.

When he died, Pastor Huber preached using the text:

"A Prince Has Fallen."
Yes he was, indeed, a prince.
Faithfully he served the Lord
In Glory he now receives his reward.
If he could speak to us today
He would say: Serve the Lord it does pay."

Chapter 6

THE DEHMELS

The Dehmels were a kind, congenial, close knit family — great to know. They were God-fearing Baptists and respected by all. There are many incidences indelibly stamped on my mind. Some good and some bad, but the good far outweighed the bad.

Grandfather Carl Dehmel Sr. was a bricklayer by trade and some of his sons followed his footsteps. He was a hard working man, but sometimes very mean. I will never forget the day we picked Grandma and Grandpa Dehmel up from the boat in Hoboken. The ravages of two World Wars were imprinted on their features as they stepped out disheartened, bent, and sad on to "The Land of the Free and the Home of the Brave."

The hardships had mellowed Grandmother, but embittered Grandfather and turned him into a cantankerous old man. He proved it, right there and then, when he argued over the pronunciation of "ice cream" which he saw advertised on the billboard. He was always right, and I never liked to play games with him because it always caused friction. He was difficult to live with and no one felt it more than his wife Louise.

The Dehmel Family

She, on the other hand, was just the reverse. Grandmother Dehmel was a gentle, quiet lady, a real mother, very loving, and understanding. However, when it came to her faith, she was too legalistic. Later in life, this had a bad effect on some of her children.

I will pick up their stories as they entwine with my life. Uncle Karl was the oldest and the first to come to America. Slowly, one by one, the other children followed, with the exception of Hermann who could not enter because of an eye problem. My father was the first to follow my Uncle Karl. We lived practically side-by-side in Elizabeth and saw much of each other. My cousins, Kate & Karl, Jr., were like siblings to me and I enjoyed being with them. Several years later my father's only sister, Augusta Dehmel Mielke, and her family joined us. Her husband's name was also Karl. Their three girls, Augusta, Martha and Elfrieda, were a challenge to me.

They rented a house on Rebecca Place, just a stone's throw from ours. Aunt Augusta, whom I called Tante Guste, converted their front room into a store and sold candy, groceries, and miscellaneous items.

I always enjoyed going there because I often received handouts. Besides, Elfrieda was my age and we were compatible. When my aunt wasn't looking, the girls would often snitch candy and give it away to their visiting friends. They became popular, but my aunt went broke and had to close the store.

Tante Guste was easy going, kind, and lovable. She was my favorite aunt. I saw her ruffled only one time. It was in the summer and she was wearing a sheer blouse. Uncle Karl, under the influence of alcohol, poked unending accusations about her wearing that blouse. Finally, she lost control, tore the blouse off and ripped it into pieces asking, "Now are you satisfied?" But she never stopped loving him. She just kept praying that God would deliver him of his bad habit.

Uncle Karl wasn't that bad. He was a lovable person and a great fisherman. He would often go out on the ocean in a large fishing boat and return with a good catch of lobster, crabs, or both. Tante Guste would then get out the old wash tub, fill it with boiling water, and call the family together for a feast. With fresh homemade bread, that was eating!

Tante Guste was also an assiduous woman. She used her hands to help with the finances that often ran short due to Uncle Karl's weakness. She worked in her own home on consignment for a factory, smocking children's dresses, sewing pillowcases, and whatever they requested. It was tedious work that did not pay too well, but it helped to supply the need. In the golden years of their lives, she became the caretaker of an apartment building, and they lived there until the death of her husband.

Tante Guste was a born-again Christian. She and the girls went to church and Sunday school faithfully. Occasionally, Uncle Karl would go with her, but his habit hindered him in serving the Lord. However, Tante Guste never gave up believing that he would get saved and be delivered from alcoholism. Her faith and endurance paid off. Several years before his death he found Jesus as his personal savior and he was completely set free from his habit. His favorite song then was: "The Old Account Was Settled Long Ago."

My day was brightened, when in my thirties, I had an unexpected visit from Tante Guste. We were pastoring a small country church in Bridgman, Michigan. No one from the Dehmel side of the family had ever stopped by, so this was exciting.

Our income, at that time, was very meager and we were not able to replace some much-needed household articles, such as, dishes, pots, linens, etc. I excused myself and used what we had. Tante Guste said, "Don't worry about it. I understand. I went through it."

That year at Christmas time, a large box arrived from Tante Guste. It was a twenty-four-piece dinner set. It wasn't cheap stuff either. It came from Goerke's, an exclusive store in Elizabeth, New Jersey. That's the kind of person Tante Guste was. I believe that she is reaping her reward in Glory today.

ANDES, NEW YORK

Uncle Karl, my father's oldest brother, came home after a hectic day. He was tired of working in a stuffy factory with its mad rush and continuous noise. He kicked off his shoes and seated himself into a comfortable ottoman while Aunt Kate prepared supper. He picked up the newspaper and wondered if he could find something

Hildegarde Dehmel Jensen

The Farm in the Catskills, Andes, N.Y. Left to right: Marie Winter, Aunt Kate Dehmel, Uncle Karl Dehmel, Mr. Winter

interesting and relaxing. To his surprise, his eyes fell on an ad, "Farm for sale in the Catskill Mountains — Andes, New York."

The more he read, the more attractive it became. Even the price was within his reach. Excitedly, he called, "Kate, come here. Read this. What would you say if we buy it?"

My aunt was reared on a ranch in Germany and understood farming from "A to Z." To her, this possibility was exciting. She loved the country and she exclaimed, "Now, Karl, you are not fooling me. Where is this place?"

"Somewhere in New York State. It can't be too far or it would not be listed in our paper. What do you say, shall I check into it?"

"Oh, yes, do," was her reply.

A few days later, they both were on their way to Andes, a town nestled in the Catskill Mountains. It was so peaceful and quiet with mountains all around. The house had many rooms and a large porch. It was in good shape as were all the other buildings. It did not take long to make a decision.

My aunt said, "Karl, I will help you pay for it. Since New York City is so close, I will convert the house into an inn and I will advertise it as a summer 'vacation spot.' The large lake to the rear of the property is just ideal for swimming and boating. Besides, I will offer the guests some good German cooking and will rent the rooms out for a week or two, or longer as desired. I will ask Johanna to come and help me during the summer months, and in that way, we'll have some extra cash to pay the farm off quickly."

This farm became my vacation spot for years to come. In fact, it became a rendezvous for the entire Dehmel family.

AN UNFORGETTABLE TRIP

I shall never forget that first trip to Andes. I was ten years old when my parents and I took the train to Jersey City. There we changed trains for upper New York State. The last stop was Margaretville. There, my Uncle Karl was to meet us with his horses and wagon.

This last stretch was the most unusual. The tracks passed through farmlands that often became troublesome. This was one of those days. The train slowed its speed, slower and slower, until it finally stopped in "no man's land." My father went to investigate and to his surprise, he saw the engineer chasing the cows off the track with a big stick. When all was clear, the train proceeded to its destination. However, our problems were just beginning.

My uncle was waiting for us when we arrived. It was a little past noon but it was getting very dark. Ominous black thunderclouds were forming overhead, and the wind began to whip up... the wagon had a top but no sides. Uncle Karl then fastened side curtains on the wagon by snapping them on, to keep us dry. My father suggested that we stay in town until the storm was over, but Uncle Karl insisted on proceeding slowly.

Andes was located on the other side of a high mountain. Therefore, the road went straight up into the storm clouds. The higher we went the more severe became the lightning, the thunder, and the downpour. The lightning crackled like a whip. It frightened the horses, and in a frenzied rush, they stampeded up the highway, tossing us from one side to the other. The tighter Uncle Karl held the reins, the more furious the horses continued their chaotic run. Would the wagon hold together? Would the wheels stay on?

We all called on God for help. He controls the weather and He could change it. Only the Almighty God could help us now. We claimed the ninety-first Psalm. "He that dwelleth in the secret place of the most High shall abide under the shadow of the Almighty...He is my refuge and my fortress: my God; in Him will I trust. Surely He shall deliver thee." — verses 1–4.

That was what we needed just then. Suddenly, the sun shown! We were above the clouds and they looked like a display of fireworks beneath us. The horses calmed down. Our problem was over. No damage had been done and we thanked God for His intervention and protection.

THE FARM

At the farm, all were waiting. As we opened the door, the aroma of the pot roast and the freshly baked rolls filled the air. My aunt was an excellent cook and her desserts and pastries always put their finishing touches on her meals.

It was, indeed, a typical farmhouse. A large wood-burning stove decked the kitchen. The stove had a water reservoir built in at the side, which was kept full and provided hot water. There was a table in the middle of the room. The cabinets were on the side with a place to put the pans to hold water. This gave them a makeshift sink.

The Farm in the Catskills House, Andes, N.Y. On the steps: Hilda and Johanna Dehmel. Standing left to right: Alvina Bailey and Augusta Mielke

Hildegarde Dehmel Jensen

HILDEGARD AND THE EGGS

One morning after breakfast, Katie handed me a small pail. She said, "Come with me, we are going to the chicken coop to gather eggs." That sounded exciting and it didn't take much coaxing.

We went from nest to nest and soon the pail was full. Then, instead of taking them to the house, Katie suggested that we go to the hayloft and look for stray nests. She led the way and I followed. As we tramped around in the freshly cut hay, Katie called out, "Watch out for the shoot! It is just in front of you."

"What is a shoot?" I asked.

"It is an opening in the floor where we throw down hay and straw for the cows below," she replied.

To make matters even worse, Uncle Karl had just brought in a load of hay and it covered the opening. I did not see it. With my toe I sampled the area around to see if the floor was firm. When I thought I had found a safe hard surface, I placed my weight on it. But alas! It was just in the center of the shoot, and down I went.

Not wanting the eggs to break, I held the bucket over my head. However, it hit the side of the shoot and capsized, covering me with eggs from head to toe. I fell all the way down and landed just in front of a stall in the barn below.

My aunt met me in the yard as I was crying and running toward the house. She took one look at me, covered completely with the yellow slimy mess, and exclaimed, "What happened to you?"

I told her of the incident. I was shaking and crying because I thought I would get punished for breaking the eggs. She replied, "Don't worry about the eggs, they can be replaced, but thank God you are not hurt." God indeed sent His angel to protect me because I came out without a scratch.

THE FAMILY TREE

Karl, the oldest, and Augusta (Gusta), the only girl in the family, are mentioned in the beginning of this chapter. My father, William, the second in line, has been projected in the "Prologue" of this book.

Hermann, the fourth oldest, was also a bricklayer. His wife, Grete, and their three children, Horst, Henry, and Marga, were the only ones who stayed in Germany. He was not permitted entry into America because of poor eyesight. Later their oldest son, Horst, followed the family here. He lived with us for a short period of time, working for my father as a mason. He married Hilde Minges and they had three children, Debbie, Ursula, and Michael.

Ernest Dehmel, the fifth in line, and his wife, Frieda, moved to Elizabeth, New Jersey in the early twenties. They had no children of their own but they adopted a little girl and named her Eleanor. She brought much happiness and sunshine to their home.

Ernest followed the electrical trade. He had a discouraging setback in his business. A friend talked him into buying a store that sold electrical products. My father sensed trouble and warned him against it. Uncle Ernest's heart was set on it and he went through with a bad deal. As the adage goes, "Not all gold glitters," and this deal went sour. He lost all his investment. It was a difficult blow, and in order to help the family over the crucial part, my parents offered for them to come and live with us until Uncle Ernest could get back on his feet.

The months they stayed with us were very pleasant. Aunt Frieda was good-hearted and good-natured, and her hands were never idle. She either had a knitting or crochet needle in her hands most of the time, and I was blessed with some of her lovely work when I was married. Eleanor was a pretty little girl, and since I had no brothers or sisters, she filled the gap.

Henry was the youngest of the Dehmel boys. He came to America with Mother and me and found the "Pot of Gold". He was employed by the Singer Sewing Machine Company and was the inventor of the Singer double needle. He worked in a glass cage locked in with his secret invention, carrying the key to that cage with him at all times. From that time on, he received top salary plus a lifetime royalty. He married a Swiss girl, Liza, and with their only child, Doris, they lived a very happy life.

Chapter 7

GERMANY

Excitement filled the air. My father broke the news that we were going to Germany. GERMANY! I had heard much about my native country and now I would get to see it.

I was seventeen years old and was holding down a typist position at Merck's in Rahway, New Jersey. It was a humdrum job, typing envelopes all day long for the Advertising Department. Now I would have a legitimate excuse to quit, and I couldn't wait—the sooner the better.

Mother and I went shopping. I bought an exquisite dress with matching shoes, hat, accessories, and numerous other outstanding pieces of clothing. I had to be the best model for the United States.

My father suggested that Mother and I go ahead of him and spend the summer visiting family and friends. He would join us in September and we would return together. The news soon spread, and two of my aunts decided to join us. So on May 7, 1927, Aunt Lise, her daughter Doris, Aunt Kate, Mother, and I left via the steamer *George Washington* from Hoboken, New Jersey.

The trip was very pleasant. The Atlantic Ocean was very calm and smooth as glass, and even Mother, who suffered seasickness, was able to enjoy the voyage on deck rather than lying in bed. For nine days we saw nothing but sky and water, but there was constant activity. The band played, people sang, deck games were offered, and besides, we never tired of listening to family fables that were often very fascinating.

At three P.M. every day, the stewards would pass out delicious mouth-watering pastries. We could choose from a variety of drinks, as well as sample the best chocolates from various countries.

Time simply flew by, and when we arrived in Bremerhafen, my mother's cousin, Lenchen Ecks, and her family welcomed us. Aunt Lise and Doris went on to Switzerland, Aunt Kate went to Muelheim, and we followed our relatives to their home in Bremen.

BREMEN

I was fascinated by the architectural style of buildings. Almost all of the houses in Bremen were either brick or cement block construction. Wooden homes were few and far between. The Ecks lived in what we'd call a brick condominium with a flight of steps leading to the front door.

As we opened the door, we were led into a spacious living room with an artistic woman's touch. The first thing that caught my eye was the "Kachel Ofen," a coral stove built into the corner of the room. It reached from wall to wall and from the floor to the ceiling. These tiles were very attractive and they sparkled and glittered. This took the place of the furnace.

Our week's stay was very pleasant. They took us sightseeing every day. All transportation was by trolley car, bicycle, or foot — so we did much walking.

There was one experience I will never forget. The Ecks had a boarder, a 38-year-old, single professor who taught at the college there. I never knew his given name. He was always addressed as "Herr Doktor," meaning Mr. Doctor. He was attracted to me from the start, but I simply despised him. He was too sissy-like for me and too old. I felt uncomfortable in his presence. I heard him say, "If she were twenty years older, she would never leave this house." I begged my mother to leave and go elsewhere, but she thought I was exaggerating.

The following day he asked me for a date. He wanted to take me on a "Hafen-rundfahrt," a drive around the harbor by boat. It always took place at night and produced a romantic atmosphere. That was the last thing I wanted and I flatly turned him down.

I cried my eyes out and finally got Mother's attention. "All right, we'll leave in the morning," she said.

That night at supper, he got up and came over to where I was sitting. What was he up to now? I could feel my heart beating. He came so close that I felt his breath against my face. He placed his arm around me and handed me a souvenir — a small, artistic cup and saucer. I breathed a sigh of relief because I feared a farewell kiss. Thank God, it didn't happen. I wanted my first and only kisses to come from whomever would eventually be my husband. That was the last encounter with Mr. Doctor.

The following day, after thanking the Ecks for their kind hospitality, we left for my mother's birthplace, Lage-Lippe. The Ecks escorted us to the depot, and we waved our good-byes until the train was out of sight.

LAGE, LIPPE

Lage, a peaceful picturesque hamlet cradled in a valley of the forest known as "Teutoburger Wald," was Mother's birthplace. Mountains completely surrounded it and tall oaks lined the main thoroughfare that led to a park in the center of town. On the outskirts flowed a sparkling, crystal-like river, and a railroad clung to its side.

As we stepped off the train, Heinrich (Henry) and Augusta Kesperling, Mother's cousin and his wife, were there to greet us. Augusta was a God-fearing, tall lanky lady with brown hair and a big smile. Her husband, Heinrich, was average in stature, cheerful, and very accommodating. He assisted with our luggage immediately and helped us carry it to their house, a short distance from the depot.

Heinrich was a plumber by trade, and together with his wife, he also owned and operated a hardware store in front of their home in the business section of town. Over the front door of their store hung a large "Welcome" sign and we felt accepted.

Mother found her equal when she sat down at their table to enjoy German hospitality. Over coffee and cake they immediately became engrossed in the word of God. Augusta told of God's guidance during the long, hard war and Mother talked about her new experience with the Holy Spirit. They burned the midnight oil and in the morning, between waiting on customers, they started all over again.

The following day Mother and I went sightseeing. She showed me the house where she was born. It was a large, two-story stone house, so different from neighboring houses. There was no monotony in styles. There were Gothic, Swiss, and typical German architectures,

Hildegarde Dehmel Jensen

Lage, Lippe Germany

and some had the house and barn attached. It was common for families to raise a pig, a goat, and a few chickens. The pig was fattened and became their meat. The goat gave them milk and butter, and the chickens provided the eggs. That was why the barn was connected to the house.

We then explored the business district. Everywhere we went there were earmarks of Mother's family. There were the hotel, a greenhouse, a florist, a shoe store, Kesperling's hardware store, a dry goods shop, and just outside the city was the large Riekehof furniture factory. They were all business people with thriving careers.

We stopped at Martha Kesperling's dry good store and made some purchases. She had the best quality of linens, and Mother stocked up. I still have some of these linens today.

RIEKEHOF'S MANSION

A pretty blond maid with a thick braid that crowned her head and a white organdy apron answered the door to our ring. With a curtsy, she asked us in and led us into a spacious living room. The furniture was of the best quality—heavy oak with hand-carved figurines. Prize-winning pictures decked the walls and pots of green foliage with bright flowers gave the room a touch of life.

Adolf Riekehof, my grandfather's brother, and his wife, Marga, joined us, welcoming us with warm caresses. It had been more than twelve years since we had last met and there was much to talk about. What a change! I was a toddler then, and now I was a young lady. Likewise, they had a son, Heinz, two years older than I, who was living at home and had just come home from work. He was learning the florist trade at the request of his father, but didn't like it. He had brought with him a large bouquet of cut flowers for the dinner table since we were to be their guests.

The dining room had a large table with matching chairs, a beautiful china closet, and a server, the best that could be bought. A crystal chandelier hung over the center of the table and the snowy white tablecloth set with the best china and the sparkling goblets glistened and brightened up the whole room.

It was a delightful meal. Course after course was served, and with it, the best of wine. I had never touched wine in my life so what was I going to do now? I did not want to hurt their feelings, so I took a sip but never finished the glass. The finishing touch was a chocolate torte—heavenly indeed.

It was a visit never to be forgotten. As we left, Heinz gave me twelve long-stemmed yellow roses. Heinz said, "Yellow stands for new love."

Heinz was such a lovely young man, but I detected an emptiness in his eyes. I wished I could have witnessed to him, but there was so much talking going on I couldn't get a word in edgewise. Shortly after getting back home, we heard that he had committed suicide. All that wealth, but without the Lord, he wasn't happy.

DETMOLD

The wind whistled ferocious through my hair. We were in a convertible, en route to Detmold, driving through Teutoburger Forest. Cars were few and convertibles even fewer. I felt ecstatic, seemingly in a dream world, as we visited the historic sites of this picturesque city in such style.

We drove past rugged old castles, antique architectural buildings, flower gardens, and parks. In one of these parks stood a gigantic statue of Hermann der Cherusker, known in Germany as "Hermann's Denkmal" (monument).

Hermann had gone to Rome and joined the army. He was a good soldier and successfully learned the army's techniques. As Napoleon was gaining in power, he went forth to conquer the

Hermann's Monument

world. Hermann fled to Germany and determined to stop Napoleon's mad rush for conquest.

Hermann settled in Lippe, Detmold, and trained a host of willing men to help him achieve his goal. He stationed these men in the hills surrounding the city. Not having enough ammunition, he equipped them with rocks, stones, clubs, and any heavy object he could find. Then, as Napoleon and his men passed through the valley below, they pelted them and completely covered Napoleon and his entire army. The army was slain and Napoleon met his Waterloo. Although he went forth conquering and to conquer he failed at Detmold in Germany. This monument stands today in honor of Hermann's great victory.

THE CATACOMB

I had heard about the "Great Persecution of the Early Christians" and the catacombs of Rome in which they met to worship the Lord their God. But I never realized that believers fled from Rome all the way to Germany, and even there, had to worship in seclusion.

Outside of Detmold there was one of these catacombs, which we visited. It was a cave hewn out of the mountain. The ceiling was very low and small shelves were cut out of the walls for lamps. That was the only light. A crude pulpit of wood stood in front and planks set on blocks served as seats. On the walls were inscribed symbols of faith, such as emblems of fish and other characters, as well as scriptures.

It was cold and damp, but a spirit of awe and worship was prevalent. The outside door was camouflaged to avoid detection.

Comparing our lives with theirs, how fortunate and blessed we are to be able to worship in beautiful comfortable edifices without fear. Yet, sad to say, many absent themselves from attending God's house because of lack of desire.

HAMBURG

It was time to move on. We were leaving Lippe and heading for the Rhineland, my birthplace. But Mother wanted to stop at Hamburg to visit her cousin.

The Rosenmeiers lived on a farm on the outskirts of the city, and when we arrived, the place was electrified with excitement. We were now Americans and what an honor it was to have us as guests.

They had a son, Willy, two years my superior, and we both connected immediately. The older folk talked and talked and we followed suit as if we were old-time pals. He wanted to know all about the United States. I could read in his eyes that he would like to explore our great nation, and he was putting out feelers right from the start to see if we would help him to make it possible.

Willy

It was now bedtime. Willy offered me his bed, but what an eye opener. The mattress was a straw tick. The following morning I felt as if I had gone through the war.

I was stiff all over, but did not complain. I wondered how Willy ever slept.

The meals were excellent. German cooking is superb. At breakfast, Willy came up with a suggestion. "Let's go to the beach today. It is going to be a hot day and I think it will be fun."

Hamburg faced the North Sea and streams of people were common there, especially when the weather was so warm. A lunch was packed and away we went. However, I did not want to go swimming. I was not prepared for that.

That day, there was an air show and one of the Sea Planes was taking up passengers. Willy wanted to go but not without me. I was afraid and refused. But he begged and pleaded and finally I consented. It was my first airplane ride. Willy held my hand as the pilot was doing somersaults. I was praying because I thought we were going to crash. What a relief when my feet were back on solid ground.

On our way home, Willy stopped to give me a treat. Ice cream was not known in Germany at that time — instead, they had whipped cream. So whipped cream was what I got. It was a large portion, and they served nothing else with it. It was so rich it made me sick. Poor Willy, he meant well. I'll never forget it.

Willy had his own motorcycle. He was so proud of it and he wanted to give me a ride. He was so disappointed when I turned him down. However, I accepted a picture of him on it, which I still have as a souvenir.

Before leaving this area, Mother wanted to visit another one of her old acquaintances. She contacted Professor Werbeck and informed him that she was on vacation from America and would like to see the family.

Arrangements were made and Mother and I were now standing at their door.

Hildegarde Dehmel Jensen

Cousin Willy took me out to a whipped cream treat.

Mr. & Mrs. Werbeck had two sons, Gustaf and Franz. The entire family welcomed us with great enthusiasm. They were interested in getting firsthand information on the lifestyle of the United States of America. Professor Werbeck had studied much about it in textbooks, but personal news was more intriguing. They devoured everything we told them like hungry birds swallowing worms.

After serving a delicious lunch, they took us sightseeing. Gustaf and Franz were just a little older than I, and I had to walk between them as they pointed out places of interest. Mother, too, was having a good time catching up on momentous occurrences of the past.

We walked through a park where there was an American Indian Village on display. There were wigwams, totem poles, canoes, and mannequins of Indians with colored feathered headdresses. The boys were so elated that they could add to their present knowledge.

However, I was secretly delighted to watch them enjoy the display.

Our last stop was at "lovers lane" down by the riverside. There was a nice wide river that flowed through the city and it drew the attention of both young and old, especially at nighttime. This area had become a center of entertainment. The colored lights, fountains, and the cafes along the broad walks were so inviting. I was fascinated by the many attractive outside eating-places. Tables and chairs were provided for eating and resting, with music for enjoyment.

We found a table, sat down, and enjoyed coffee and some delicious teacakes. I was intrigued by the river in the twilight. It was a fun place to be and I enjoyed it. When it was time, it was sad to say good-bye, but we had to move on.

MUELHEIM A/D RUHR

As we approached the Fischer home, where we were to stay for the duration of our visit in Muelheim, we were surprised by our reception. Over the front door of their brick home was a large "Welcome" sign. Karl Jr., the oldest son, and Walter, his brother, met us to assist us with our luggage. Lischen, their ten year daughter, was looking through the window, and Lina, Mother's longtime bosom friend was standing in the doorway holding a bouquet of flowers. Her husband, Karl Sr., was waving excitedly. You see, Mother played "Cupid" for these two, and her interest in them was never forgotten.

Karl Fischer, Sr. was a tailor by trade. In those days suits were not purchased in department stores, but men went to professional tailors for fittings. Karl, Sr. was a small man and it was interesting to see him sitting cross-legged on his "tailor table" stitching away on the suits.

Hildegarde Dehmel Jensen

Muelheim A/D RUHR

He worked out of his own house and I had the benefit of watching him.

Lina, his wife, was also small in stature. She was a perfect hostess—kind, congenial, and very pleasant. She was the kind of person anyone would be proud to know.

Karl Jr., was studying at the University, preparing himself to become a chemical engineer. He was blond, blue eyed, and slim—every girl's dream. Although the family were devout, God-fearing Baptists, I noticed that the seeds of Communism planted by his professors were taking effect. His parents noticed it too, and they were very concerned. I spoke to him in length about the truth of the Gospel, but he needed constant strengthening in his faith. Doubt had been planted and it was germinating. I would not be able to give him the faith-building help he needed since I would be leaving.

When we parted he asked permission to write me. He said, "I will write you in English, and please correct my mistakes, and you write me in German, and I will do likewise." This we did for a short time only, and then he married and moved to Russia.

MY BIRTHPLACE

Mother then took me to the house where I was born. It was a three-story apartment building in the elite part of the city known as, "The Poet's Section." At the end of our street was a park with a bubbling fountain. To the rear was the "First Pentecostal Church," also known as the Stone Street Church.

The church was buzzing with excitement, and since we had time, we stopped for a service. Worshippers swarmed in like a bunch of bees, and we joined them. As we entered the church we felt the awesome presence of God. It was like the dew of Herman that King David talked about in Psalms 133:3. The church was quite full but we found two places and seated ourselves. The singing was electrifying. Not only were lips moving, the words seemed to break forth with inner, heartfelt emotion. It was refreshing, like coming out of the desert to an oasis of clear sparkling water, or out of the wilderness into the presence of God Jehovah like Moses experienced at the Burning Bush.

A young lady stood up and gave a prophecy. She said, "I see a road. For some it is too narrow, for others too rocky and steep, but for some challenging." She then sat down.

There were three ministers on the platform, and one of them rose, took his Bible, and opened up to Proverbs 14:12, reading: "There is a way which seemeth right unto a man, but the end thereof are the ways of death."

He then expounded on the reasoning and the desire of man to take the easy road and he referred to Matthew 7: 13, 14. "Enter ye in at the strait gate: for wide is the gate, and broad is the way, that leadeth to destruction, and many there be which go in there at: because strait is the gate, and narrow is the way, which leadeth unto life, and few there be that find it."

This wide road is easy to travel because it is convenient, and you can live as you please, but this road — this life-style — leads to destruction. The narrow road is not the majority's choice because excess baggage must be stripped. There is no room for it. But many people do not want to give it up. Yet this is the road that leads to life everlasting. It was a decision-making service and several went forward to make a total commitment.

MY EIGHTEENTH BIRTHDAY

My parents always placed great value on celebrating my birthdays — perhaps because I was an only child. This day wasn't any different. My father had arrived from America and my mother made arrangements with Rosa to give me a birthday party.

It was so good to see my Aunt Greta Dehmel. She was such a precious person, but because of my uncle's eye problem, the United States would not grant them entrance. Therefore, she and her family were separated from the rest of the family by so many miles of great ocean.

This birthday party was something like a family reunion. My two aunts and cousin, who came on the trip, were able to be there. It was a gala occasion and Hilda Schaumkessel, my namesake, kept us entertained with her guitar and song.

We had one advantage — we were all of one faith, and the evening ended as we all worshiped the Lord together. For some of us it was a final farewell, but only here on

A CONTINUOUS MIRACLE

Two Hilda's making music.

earth. We all had the hope of meeting again in the "land of endless day."

KOBLENZ

The mighty Rhine, like the Mississippi, flowed majestically through Germany. This river reminded me of the Hudson in Upper New York State because of its attractive "vineyards" along its banks. Dotted between greenery were castles that gave the river a touch of chivalry.

As I stood at the banks of this stately popular river, I was not only overwhelmed by its splendor, but by the many boats and barge activities which at this point changed into river commerce. It was interesting to see these large barges being pulled instead of pushed, as we do in our country.

I was startled out of my seemingly dream world, by the chimes of the Koelner Dom (Cologne Cathedral), a magnificent church just a short distance behind me. This church was a masterpiece of art, inside and out. I stood in awe of its massive stained glass window, tall ceiling, and many artistic statues.

It was also famous for its tall steeple and the unusual clock in the tower. The clock was similar to a cuckoo clock with one exception. Instead of a cuckoo appearing every hour, every one of the twelve apostles appeared. At the strike of every hour they would appear in rotation, one after the other. Everyone had to stop to see this event. Truly, God and man can accomplish much to make life meaningful.

BERLIN

The alarm woke me out of a deep sleep. It was still dark and I wondered why it rang. I jumped up to turn it off—and then I remembered. We were catching an early train to Berlin.

Berlin was the capital of Germany at that time, and Mother wanted me to see it. She had connections. The parents of Jose and Martha Gartner, whom Mother met in Lebanon, New Jersey, lived there. They had given Mother some gifts to take to their parents, and that gave us an open door to visit.

As a backdrop, class distinction at that time was an important factor throughout all of Germany. For example: First class—the very wealthy, Second class—the elite, Third class—the middle class, and Fourth class—the poor and the farmers.

This day, we were traveling "Fourth Class," for my benefit. Mother wanted me to see what it was like, and it was an eye opener. The train had ten coaches. Fourth class was the last coach. It was a boxcar with benches on all four sides, similar to our park benches, with a large empty space in the center.

We boarded and sat on one of these seats. Within minutes, everything was buzzing with activity. The farmers on their way to market brought their chickens, cases of eggs, vegetables, plus live stock—even some pigs. The roosters crowed, the pigs grunted, and soon that center was so crowded, that we were squeezed like an accordion, and were glad when we reached our destination.

Since the Gartners were older people, they did not meet us at the depot. Instead, we took a streetcar, and got off close to their house. It was a small ranch-style house just outside of the city limits, with a white picket fence around it. It sat back a little from the street and was surrounded by various kinds of fruit trees.

They were expecting us and gave us a warm welcome. There was no end of questions as to how their girls were doing. They were congenial, pleasant, and God-fearing. They asked us to stay over-night and offered us a room, which we accepted. That made it possible for Mother to show me the city the following day.

Our first stop was at Potsdam, the chancellor's mansion. There were approximately ten steps going up to it, and each step contained a garden of flowers and shrubs. These were accented with spraying fountains. It was breath taking, and the fragrance of the flowers scented the entire air.

Our next stop was the Brandenburg Gate, a turning point between East and West where so many political decisions took place. At that time it did not mean as much as it does today. It was simply an architectural masterpiece.

We took the train, third class, back to Fischer's, which was our headquarters while we were visiting in Muelheim. Third class was also a different way of traveling. One car was divided into four closed sections with a door on each side. There were two rows of seats facing each other. Second class was similar to our coaches, and first class was like ours. The trains ran very smoothly and fast. We were glad to get back so we could rest.

OBERHAUSEN

Oberhausen, a twin city of Muelheim, was the heart of Germany's steel industry. The massive factories with their smoke stacks left the city, most of the time, in a haze of smog. It was not the best place to live, but the lucrative income outweighed the disadvantages.

We had come to visit the Theissen family. I was especially interested in meeting Grete. Eric Loenser, one of our young people, had spoken so much about her, and I wondered who she was.

I rang the doorbell and a beautiful, shy young lady answered. She blushed slightly when we introduced ourselves and asked us in. Her mother appeared and gave us a warm welcome. At this point, I did not know how close Grete and I would some day become.

Mrs. Theissen was a somewhat heavyset woman with dark hair and large sparkling eyes. She greeted us with a pleasant, motherly handshake—the kind one can never forget. We were seated in a large living room with a feminine touch. In the corner stood an organ with an enlarged picture of Eric on it. I commented, "That's a nice picture of Eric and he sends you his greeting."

She replied, "Thank you. He gave it to me together with his organ when he left for America." I then put two and two together and understood why he wanted us to visit her.

Grete's father, Reverend Theissen, was the pastor of the local Pentecostal church. He was loved and respected by all. He always planned some interesting activities for his young people, and while we were visiting, he invited me to join their Youth Group on an outing they were having the following day. With Mother's permission, I accepted. It was a rewarding experience.

All forests in Germany were government controlled. They were preserved, cared for, and kept clean from underbrush and weeds by state-appointed foresters. A path was provided through the woods for strolling and bicycling. At appointed places, cabins were provided as comfort areas. These were referred to as "Jungend Herberge." These were pleasant places to stop, rest, and snack.

This day, the youth group was taking a trip on this path. They started at church in a procession with guitars and song. Happily they went singing to their hearts' content. Of course, humor and teasing were thrown in. It was a fun day. We stopped at the "Herberge," rested, and then returned just in time to take in the evening service. It was good wholesome fun and I thoroughly enjoyed it.

I was Grete's partner in this march and she shared some of her deep inner feelings with me. I sensed that she was deeply in love with Eric, and I determined that when I got back home I would confront Eric with it. I also discovered that she was deeply devoted to the Lord and it was easy to converse with her about spiritual matters. I was glad that I met her for she was sweet and a pleasure to know.

Father had obligations to meet and we had to bring our vacation to a close. We were soon boarding the ship, *Lutzuf*, on the Atlantic Ocean. It was difficult to say goodbye, and amidst a cloud of waves, we gradually drifted out of sight.

Hildegarde Dehmel Jensen

THE STORM

On the boat going home to America. Center standing: Wilhelm Dehmel with daughter Hilde Dehmel on right and two friends.

Our return trip was unforgettable. My aunts and cousin met us at Bremerhafen where, together, we boarded the steamer *Lutzuf*. It was a tourist boat for second and third class passengers. We were returning in the middle of October and hoped for good weather, however, it was not to be.

The first few days were enjoyable but then we hit a hurricane coming from the South Atlantic. *Lutzuf* was a smaller boat and much shorter than the average steamer. It bounced on the waves like a matchbox.

The sky became black, the rain came down in torrents, and the wind blew as if it would tear everything apart. The steamer tilted, the ocean covered the deck, and it felt as if the steamer would capsize. The boat workers ran to let down the awnings on the side of the deck to keep the water out. It was difficult for them to keep their footing. Everyone was afraid, even the captain turned pale as a loud crash startled him. He immediately gave orders for the anchors to be cast.

In the dining room all meals were suspended and a railing was placed around the tables to keep the contents

1927, A storm on the Atlantic Ocean taken from the Ocean Liner **Lutzuf** *by its captain.*

from sliding to the floor. Only sandwiches were served for those who were not seasick.

Fear gripped me and I went to my cabin, got on my knees, and had a talk with my Lord. I felt very much like Paul must have felt on his voyage to Rome in Acts 27:22-24. "I exhort you to be of good cheer: for there shall be no loss of any man's life among you... For there stood by me this night the angel of God, whose I am and whom I serve, saying, Fear not."

Then a chorus flashed into my mind:

"Sweetly I rest in the arms of my Savior
Nothing to fear while in Him I abide."

Immediately a peace overshadowed me and all fear was gone. It stormed all night but joy came in the morning. The wind ceased, the sun came out, and everyone breathed easier.

As our boat pulled into dock a few days later, all was forgotten, and we were greeted by a host of friends who had come to welcome us home. My mother's mother, her brother, and friends from our church, including Eric, were there to greet us. Eric asked about Grete and I injected, "Don't forget her. You made some promises to her, keep them." We then talked about the storm and thanked God for His keeping power.

There is a song that says, "The anchor holds in spite of the storm." How true that also is in the "Spiritual Life." Whenever we take Jesus as our anchor we will survive all storms of life.

Friends waiting for the Steamer Lutzuf to dock, welcoming home (to the USA) Wilhelm, Johanna, and Hilde Dehmel.

Short Stories

TEN-CENT RING

December thirtieth had come. It was my wedding day. Jumping out of bed I rushed to the window to see what the weather had to offer. The sky was gray with mountains of threatening clouds. Would there be more snow added to the already sparkling blanket covering the ground? It looked like a mason gone mad. The snow stuccoed bushes and evergreens into grotesque pyramids. It looked uninvitingly cold, but the tracks of our friendly squirrel proved he didn't care as long as he found food. He had become so tame that, in the summer months, he would eat out of our hands and, in the winter, came begging at our kitchen window.

The aroma of freshly perked coffee filled the air. I rushed downstairs to join Mother and Alvina, a friend who had come to lend a helping hand.

I'll never forget the day Alvina and I met. Answering the chimes of the doorbell, there stood this stranger asking for Johanna Dehmel. She spoke loudly, seemed very forward, and her personality clashed with mine. However I invited her in, called Mother, and then eavesdropped.

A CONTINUOUS MIRACLE

The introduction was amazing. She had just arrived from Germany, was a total stranger in America, and the only contact name she had was Mother's. Mother's name had been given to her by her sister who, years prior, had worked for the same people Mother had.

My mother was a kind generous person who always bent backwards to help someone, so of course Alvina Hoff came to stay at our house. As the saying goes, "you can never know the meat of the nut by its shell," so likewise I misjudged Alvina by her initiation. She had been an army nurse, which accounted for her boldness. I later found her to be kind, warm, considerate, brilliant, and everything one would look for in a true friend.

I was only a teenager then. As years passed, she married a charming minister, and came to assist me in this big event. She had baked, cooked, and with the help of another friend, Louise Misteli, had catered the entire wedding.

Alfred, or Al, my husband-to-be, was studying at Southwestern Bible College in Enid, Oklahoma. He had come home for the Christmas holidays. He was tall, blonde, and handsome—the answer to a maiden's prayer. We had been engaged for some time and were madly in love, but had postponed our marriage until he graduated.

In the meantime, I was working as a secretary for a manufacturing firm in New Jersey. Miles had separated us and correspondence was the only means of communication. Since our letters had been intercepted, and in order to avoid further disruptions and misunderstandings both at school and at home, we decided to get married and settle it. That left us only ten days for preparations.

Being an only child, a flimsy wedding wouldn't do. It had to be in style, not flashy, but moderate. My dad had his own contracting business, but the Nineteen Thirty depression had hit him hard. When he went to collect for work he had done, there was no money forthcoming. This put him into a terrific bind just when we needed money most. He was conservative and a good planner, so he and Mother figured out a way to have the kind of wedding for me that fit in their budget.

We had a lovely brick home with a large basement. With the help of young people at church, the basement got a quick face-lift and soon was transformed into an attractive banquet hall accommodating eighty guests.

Al had given me a beautiful diamond ring but had not yet purchased the complete set. Now he had to buy the wedding band. Dad had a friend who was in the jewelry business, and at Dad's request, we looked up Mr. Wilnus. He could offer us what we wanted, a plain band with six diamond chips. However, he did not have it in stock, but promised to have it in time for the occasion.

A friend of Mother's, an excellent seamstress, made my gown as a wedding gift. The gown was white silk with a lace neckline. There were small buttons down the back of the dress and on the sleeves from elbow to wrist—precisely what I wanted.

The Maid of Honor and bridesmaids were successful in purchasing matching velvet gowns, and the flower girl was primped up to correspond with both. Invitations had been printed and mailed in time, but a few things remained for the last day, and it was now here.

Dad drove me to church where I was to meet Alfred. Together we were going to put the finishing touches on the decorations—but alas!—He didn't show up. The bitter cold weather, plus exertion from answering SOS calls to dig friends out of the snow the day before, grounded him in bed with a fever. What were we to do now? Could we go through with the ceremony? Would he be well by then?

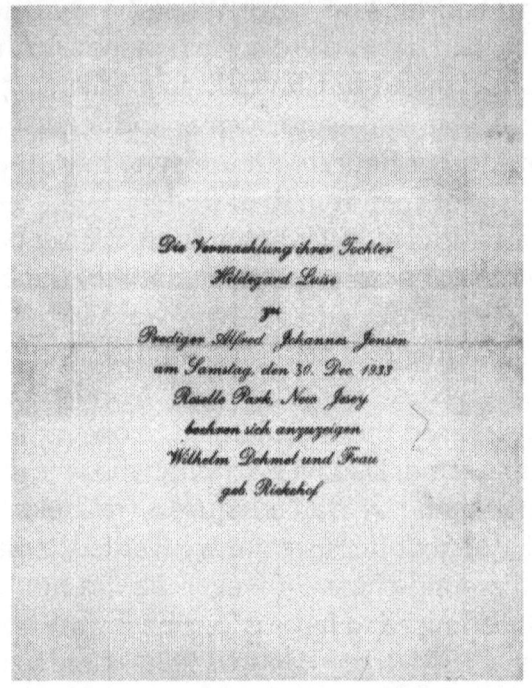

December 30, 1933, Wedding Invitation for Hildegard Dehmel's marriage to Alfred Jensen.

We had prepared a full-course meal: chicken with all the trimmings, numerous salads, and for dessert, not only the wedding cake, but a variety of others as well. What would we do with all this food and with the out-of-town guests? I felt my nerves tightening, but a good cry coupled with prayer brought relief.

In full faith that all would work out, I proceeded with the church decorations alone. When all was finished, I viewed my work with satisfaction. The rays of sun upon the glistening snow reflected through the stained-glass windows as a mirage of northern lights, and flooded the chapel with a glow that brought new hope for the future.

As I stood there meditating in absolute quiet, the silence was suddenly broken by the voice of the pastor's wife, Mrs. Kalis, who lived adjacent to the church. "I just had a phone call from your mother. She wondered if you had ordered the flowers."

Oh no! I had forgotten. "What shall I do now?" I asked. "I have no car and the florist is some distance away — and only seven hours before the wedding."

Placing her arm gently around me, she said, "Don't worry, I'll drive you over."

Her answer was like a breath of fresh air, and as we walked into the flower shop, it was like coming out of a storm into a haven of calm.

I placed an order for six white chrysanthemums for the bridal bouquet, six each of rust and gold for the attendants, a basket of petals for the flower girl, boutonnieres for the men, a corsage for Mother, and flowers for the altar. It was a large order but I was fortunate, they were not busy and were able to deliver the flowers on time.

As I closed the door of the shop, whom should I run into but Mother. She had been so busy making preparations that she forgot to buy her dress.

"Please go with me and help me pick it out," she pleaded."

"I can't. I haven't time," I replied.

It was already past noon, and certainly no time to go shopping. But I weakened, and the next hour or so found us rushing from one dress shop to another looking for something appropriate. I had not eaten and I was hungry. But I was too excited to eat and we had no time. If only we could find what we were looking for — and there it was: a soft gray crepe with lace trimming. It fit like a glove. We made the purchase and I saw Mother off on the bus. Then I went to the Beauty Shoppe.

This was a first for me. Hairdressing had just been introduced, and I was naive. I asked for a wash and set without an appointment and was told to be seated and wait. I picked up a magazine, sat down, and fingered through it. I watched the minutes of the clock on the wall tick away while my mind was agitating like a butter churn. That was it. I could wait no longer. I got up to leave when I heard my name called. My hair was long, which didn't help the situation any. The beautician was kind and soon had me under the dryer. However, it was getting late. I crawled out from under the dryer and said, "Comb me out, if I'm dry or not, for I must be to my wedding by seven o'clock."

The girl almost fainted and replied, "Why didn't you tell me sooner?" With the help of a pro they had me ready to go in short order.

The heavy snow and the five o'clock rush hour had completely paralyzed traffic. How to get home was another problem. It had to be by way of the bus. It seemed like an eternity before one came, and then, it was too crowded to stop. Suddenly, I remembered that we had no wedding ring. Mr. Wilnus had not kept his promise.

An idea flashed through my mind. Why not run across the street to the Dime Store, and pick up a ten-cent ring? It would do for an emergency. As quick as a whistle, I dashed across the street, made the purchase, and rushed back just as a bus came into full view. It stopped long enough to let off one passenger; I grabbed the handrail, stepped up, and hung on as the bus pulled away from the curb. Partly dangling, partly standing, but with grim determination to make it, I succeeded.

It was almost six o'clock when I got home. Mother met me at the door exclaiming, "Where have you been."

The irony of it all was that both of my attendants were waiting, fully dressed, and I the bride, was just coming in. "Hurry up," Mother then said. "The wedding is going off as planned. Alfred called and he is feeling better."

I took two steps at a time up a flight of stairs, and in less than half an hour, was ready for church. Glancing into the mirror I eyed myself with satisfaction. I was dressed traditionally in "something old, something new, something borrowed, and something blue." But little did I know the tears this borrowed veil would bring.

A dear friend offered to lend me her veil, and since money was scarce, I accepted the offer. However, it had been stored in a box for several years and had become brittle.

Dad's Hupmobile was standing in the driveway ready for take off. It was his pride and joy. Dad was 5'7", weighed 175 pounds, had brown hair, sky blue eyes, and a little mustache that he pampered. He carried himself well, as always looking as if he were ready for display. He had been an officer in the army and had remained a soldier at heart. He never lost his identity. He was so meticulous that he could see the tiniest speck at a glance, a book out of order on a shelf, the unwashed cup in the sink, and the unwanted fingerprints on the steering wheel of his car. Nothing escaped his eagle eye. Really, he was as fussy as an "old maid" — he was the perfectionist.

We were just ready to step into the car when unexpectedly as a bomb, an argument exploded. This was certainly not the time or the place for an episode of this kind. It all centered on Aunt Kate.

Aunt Kate had come a hundred and seventy miles from the Catskills for the occasion, and she was depending on us for transportation to the church. Alfred's brother Otto, the best man, was to pick up the bridal party at our house, but he didn't show up. It was absolutely impossible for my Dad to take us all in his car, so Dad suggested that Aunt Kate take the bus. That's when it all started.

Aunt Kate was a jolly old soul whom everyone liked—if for no other reason that the farm, which she and Uncle Karl owned, was a perfect vacation spot. I suppose she was often taken advantage of. Her good cooking—the handsome rolls were as tempting as cheese was to mice—the wide open country, the crystal clear stream of water flowing just below the house, plus the lake that was an excellent swimming spot just over the hill, were all drawing factors for all the city folk. No sooner would a car pull up behind the house then Aunt Kate could be heard poking up the fire, putting on the coffee pot, and getting ready to greet the guests.

However, there was another side of her that was not as pleasant, yet could be humorous. When she would get upset, profanity flowed like a river. However, when an electrical storm brewed overhead, she suddenly became pious and began praying. Then she would run to the basement stairs and hide till all was over.

Right now she was simply beside herself and burst out saying, "I've come all the way from the Catskills to see you get married and I'll miss it all. I'll never forgive you for this."

"Very well then," I replied. "We'll all wait." And, wait we did.

The chapel was filled with guests. Alfred and his party were waiting, groomed in tuxedoes. We had not planned this, but he wanted to surprise me. He kept watching the door, but there was no sign of his bride. The suspense was too much for him, and with permission, he used the pastor's phone to give me a call.

The tension at home was sharply interrupted by the ringing of the phone.

I answered it, "Hello."

"Hilda, is that you?" Alfred asked.

"Yes," I replied.

"What's happened? Have you deserted me?" he questioned.

"No dear, but there is a transportation problem. Where is Otto? Why didn't he come to pick Aunt Kate up?"

"Oh, Honey, call a taxi. That should do it."

"A cab! Thanks." Why had I not thought of that?

I called the cab, but Aunt Kate would not let us go until the cab had picked her up.

The ride to the church was the most sickening I ever had. Every time I turned my head my veil ripped. I sat like a glass doll in a china shop holding my breath. Still, it tore more. I began sobbing. What would Martha, who so very kindly loaned me her cherished veil, say? Talk about mixed emotions — I had them.

Thus, an hour late, the bridal procession began with a weeping bride, a distressed Mother, and a Dad who, wiping the tears, did all he could do to comfort and cheer.

The church was crowded. Starting down the aisle, hanging on Dad's arm, stimulated with excitement, I forgot my problems. Tears vanished and were replaced with accelerated joy as I got a glimpse of my beloved looking so sharp in his tuxedo.

The ceremony began. I was shaking from sheer exhaustion. Alfred stood there so stately and calm, but his turn was next, for when Pastor Kalis asked, "What token do you have?" he suddenly remembered he had forgotten the ring. This was my moment of triumph. Reaching for his hand I gave him the ten-cent ring, which he quickly passed on to the Best Man, who in turn gave it to the Minister, who gave it back to Alfred to slip on my finger. It went so smoothly that even Reverend Kalis did not know what had happened.

It was a solemn moment as we knelt before God in His presence exchanging our sacred vows. My heart prayed, "Spare our lives from the confusion of the day, and be a guiding light down the pathway of time."

The way out of church was more joyful. At the back of the church we responded to the greetings of friends wishing God speed. Congratulation kisses and favorable comments over my pretty wedding ring were plenteous — if they had only known. Deception is cheap. It taught me a real lesson that I never forgot.

As the front doors opened, we rushed for the car waiting for us. Alfred, as a gesture of protection, gently covered my face with his derby to shield me from the rice and snowballs that were coming in my direction.

The streetcar tracks in front of the church had been cleared all day from the snow, leaving a two-foot embankment, an elevation I had failed to figure on. As I proceeded to step into the car, which was lower than I, I did not stoop down far enough and I hit my head severely against the top of the car. I felt it crack. I felt the hot blood rush into that spot. The pain was terrific and I became nauseous and deathly sick. Alfred took me into his arms, and as I cuddled close to him, he supported my head on his chest.

Alfred was a man of faith. He had seen many healed by the power of God and now was no exception. He immediately called on God for healing, and instantly I felt a warm relaxing sensation come over me. The pain lessened, and I felt greatly relieved. I thanked Alfred for his prayer, and God for his intervention.

Eighty guests gathered for the reception. Martha, the friend who loaned me the veil, assured me that she understood and urged me not to worry. The real ring replaced the ten-cent wedding ring, but our love never had to be replaced. After fifty years, it is still loyal, strong, and true.

Wedding of Alfred and Hilda Jensen. From left to right: Unknown Groomsman (standing in for Willy Jensen who died), Best Man Otto Jensen, Groom Alfred John Jensen, Bride Hildegard E. Dehmel Jensen, Maid of Honor Ruth Eckler. On far right: Ruth Finnern. Flower Girl: Ruth Dedecius

A CONTINUOUS MIRACLE

LOVEST THOU ME MORE?

A true story by Hildegard Dehmel Jensen. Published in the weekly pamphlet, LIVE, *December 1, 1991, Gospel Publishing House, Springfield, Mo.*

It was one of those cold, blustering, snowy days in northern Wisconsin, typical of their December weather. My husband, a graduate of Southwestern Bible College, had recently accepted the call to pastor a church in Athens, a farming community.

The people were kind, caring, and hospitable. It was not unusual for them to stop at our house and shower us with goodies from their farms. Although our salary was meager and our living quarters were indigent, we thanked God for what we had and for the opportunity of serving Him.

It was our third Christmas together, and God had given us a little girl, whom we named Ruth. She filled our lives with sunshine, and at 22 months old, we looked forward to an exciting Christmas. We had already received a package from my folks in New Jersey, with so many lovely gifts that we personally could not have provided. We were assured of a bright

Christmas, however, like Peter in John 18:27, we were not aware of the test just around the corner.

Ruth was not herself. She had lost her perkiness and had developed a cough, which we believed was just a cold. Her condition grew worse, and when her temperature climbed, we consulted with a doctor who diagnosed her condition as "double pneumonia." (This was in 1936, before penicillin was available.)

Looking at us, he said, "Sorry, her condition is advanced, and I cannot guarantee her recovery. I can do one thing. I can give her a shot and within 48 hours we will know one way or the other. She will either die or survive."

Looking at the doctor, I asked, "May we give God the benefit of the doubt?"

He replied, "Certainly, I am a God fearing man, and if you choose to take that avenue, do so. But please, let me know the result. Before you go I will give you some helpful instructions. Keep her in a room with the window slightly open to give her fresh air and keep the temperature at 70 degrees. Don't move her. Let her lie very still. She will then have a better chance to get well."

The following two days were hectic. We had no phone and as the crisis neared, Alfred went to a minister friend, asking for assistance in prayer. While Alfred was gone, the crisis came. I had been in constant prayer but was not aware of the test before me.

As I approached her bed, the first glance frightened me. She did not seem to be breathing. Hysteria overtook me. I picked her up, shook her, and took her into the living room, laying her on the couch—right next to a red-hot, potbelly stove. I went to the window, and looking at the sky I cried, "Lord, don't let me see her die. Please give her back to me."

At this point I heard an audible voice questioning, "Lovest thou Me more than her?"

What would I answer? If I would say, "I love You more than her," then He would perhaps say, "Let Me have her." If I replied, "I love her more than You," He might answer, "You are not worthy of Me." I could not live with that.

At that vulnerable moment, Satan stepped into the picture. The battle commenced. I heard Satan's false accusations, "See? That's what you get for serving the Lord faithfully. He is a bad paymaster." Instantly, Satan strung before me a line on which hung all the gifts that were in the Christmas package—the little doll, the big ball, the pretty dress, etc. To make it even worse, Satan threatened that she would never be able to play with those things nor wear the beautiful dress that she would only wear in the casket. The continuing accusations tempted me sorely, but I recognized Satan's schemes.

The Lord had done so many wonderful things for me in the past, how could I let Him down now? Never, even if I had to make the same commitment that Abraham made. I could live without Ruth but I could not live without the Lord.

Again, looking into the sky, I replied, "I love You more than her. If You want her, please take her."

I went back to the couch where she lay. I felt her face. It seemed so cold. I picked up her hand and it fell limp. Looking to the Lord, I asked, "Please Lord, give me the strength to tell Alfred when he returns that Ruth is with You."

Then, I heard the same voice in clear tender words say, "Take back your Isaac."

I looked down at Ruth again as she opened her eyes and smiled. Her fever had disappeared. Ruth was healed.

Hildegarde Dehmel Jensen

Mother and daughter: Hildegard Dehmel Jensen and Ruth Jensen Orewiler.

God had given a Christmas miracle to us. We still have our Ruth today.

ANGELS IN DISGUISE

It was a cold day in mid-winter and we were pastoring in Scottsbluff, Nebraska. Alfred, my husband, had just brought in the mail and he was holding an odd-looking postcard in his hand. There was something strange about this card. It appeared to have been duplicated, and it had an odd request.

"Please send an anointed handkerchief. My wife is very ill with a tumor and needs prayer."

The address and signature were almost illegible, but after closer scrutiny Al deciphered it as a place in a remote area outside of our city. Turning to me he said, "Let's drive over and see what's up—I'm afraid my letter may never reach them, and she may be in desperate need of help. Bundle Ruth up and come with me."

"Are you out of your mind?" I asked. "Who would take a two-year old child out in this weather on a wild goose chase? You could get stuck in the snow and what then?"

But Alfred would not accept no for an answer. He was very determined and I knew it was futile to try to change his mind. Thus an hour later the Jensens were struggling to keep the car on an unplowed country road with no houses in sight.

Proceeding slowly, we passed a mailbox with the same name on it as that on the card, but we saw no house. Alfred said, "Someone does live here for there are footprints leading from the mail box to the rear." Looking again, we saw a curl of smoke coming from a chimney protruding about three feet behind a mound of snow. Nothing else was visible. Alfred said, "I didn't come this far to be defeated. I'm going to drive to that house."

"And how are you going to do that on a field of snow without a road?" I asked.

"Just watch me," he replied. He had a good Ford with snow tires and was over-confident. Turning off, he began to follow the footprints. At first it appeared as if he would succeed, but then suddenly, he sank into a three-foot snowdrift. Having come prepared, he got out his shovel and began digging. But try as he might, each time he started the motor, the car only spun from one side to the other.

There we were in the middle of a sea of snow with no one to turn to for help. But GOD, the OMNISCIENT and OMNIPRESENT ONE, saw our plight and came to our assistance. He saw the sincerity and concern of Alfred's heart and did not forget us.

Suddenly, out of nowhere, came a Cadillac with three elegantly dressed men. Later we discovered them to be clergymen from neighboring churches. They stopped and one of the men stepped out, calling, "Do you need help? Let me drive you out. I'm a pro at such things." Relieved, my husband gave him the wheel, and in no time we were back on the road.

We were then asked, "Please, tell us what brought you here." Alfred then identified himself, and fumbling for the postcard, pulled it out of his pocket and handed it to them.

Perplexed, Rev. Dove, who had pulled us out, looked at it and said, "That is strange. Each one of us has received the same identical card."

At this point curiosity reached its climax and all decided to find out the secret behind it. Rev. Dove then suggested that we all get into his Cadillac and he would drive us there. "I'm familiar with this area. I am acquainted with the ridges and the air current, and I can get there without any problem"

As we reached the top of the ridge and looked down, we saw a most unbelievable sight. The entire house was sandbagged up to the second story windows. There were two windows and out of one protruded a rifle. Several ferocious dogs made our presence known and came running toward the car. An ominous feeling came over me and I breathed a silent prayer for protection. We had been spotted and there was no turning back.

The door opened and a short, bald-headed man with protruding nose, dressed in overalls and sweater came toward us. "Who are you and what do you want?" he questioned.

Rev. Dove, acting as spokesman, conveyed the purpose of our coming. "We received your cards and have come to pray for the sick one."

After eyeing us over, the man asked us in. We got out of the car and Rev. Dove cautioned Ruth and me to stay in the middle of the pastors so they could keep an eye on us. What we were then to see came as a further shock.

A skinny, five-foot fellow, about 40 years old, with an apron tied around him came out of the kitchen. He too looked suspiciously at us from the top of his glasses that had fallen to the bottom of his nose. He wiped his hands on his apron and could easily have been linked to one of Al Capone's crowd. Two other curious-looking men made their appearance. Each of them kept guarding and watching a large glass cage, which was under lock and key, and had several shelves of what looked to me like every kind of money printed in the world. I would have liked to take a closer look, but we were all quickly ushered into a dim bedroom where a very heavy-set lady lay in bed. Her stomach protruded visibly under the covers. It was so unnaturally large; it must have been artificially produced.

It was now time for prayer. Alfred was chosen. I think the other ministers were afraid to close their eyes. After prayer we left quickly, not daring to take a second look at the rare display of currency.

Everyone breathed a sigh of relief after getting back on the road. We had discovered the secret. A counterfeit money ring was our guess. We speculated that the handkerchiefs, which were made of a fine fabric, produced a better grade of money.

I believe that God sent the clergymen at that exact time, AS ANGLES IN DISGUISE to protect us. Had we succeeded in getting there by ourselves, I believe we would never have returned to tell the story.

I believe we personally experienced PSALMS 91:11 — "For he shall give his angels charge over thee, to keep thee in all thy ways."

Epilogue

The men went to the police and were told to keep the event quiet and only between themselves. Their safety would be uncertain if their finding was revealed. They also believed that the woman posing as having had a tumor had probably stuffed a pillow on her stomach under the blankets to make the ministers think she was really ill.

PROGRESSION AT THE BIG PRAIRIE, A.G. CAMP
William and Johanna Dehmel — as Caretakers

For some time now, I have been impressed to write about the 15 years of my parents' stay as "Caretakers" of our Assemblies of God campground in Big Prairie, Ohio. All the training and experiences Dad had through his life prepared him for what he accomplished at Big Prairie camp.

We were pastoring the Immanuel Church on Wayne Street and had transferred from the German Branch into the English. It was then that my husband heard that they were looking for a Caretaker for the camp. Up until that time, Estelle Maffat, who owned a cottage on Route 100 just opposite the camp had been asked to keep an eye on the property. She was a part-time caretaker, but as our camp grew, the need for a full-time person was realized. Alfred, my husband, felt that my father would be good for that position. He then contacted my father and asked if he would be interested. After praying about it,

Caretakers of Big Prairie Camp William and Johanna Dehmel

my parents felt the guidance of the Holy Spirit to take that step.

My father had been a contractor for many years in New Jersey. Later, while in Michigan, he worked as a machinist and was introduced to pipes and hardware. Years ago, during the Depression, he worked at a store and learned how to make window shades and keys. Little did he realize, at that time, that God was preparing him to use these skills later in life. Thus, we felt that he was well qualified for this work.

In the late spring of 1950, Father came for an interview with Brother Van Meter and the Camp board. Everyone seemed well pleased but there was some concern about his age. He was 70 years old at the time. When Brother Van Meter asked him if he could handle it, he answered with a question. "Do you think I am a baby?" After a good laugh, he was hired. He needed some time to sell his house in Michigan. But, God brought it to a quick conclusion and in September of that year they moved into the Anderson Cottage in Big Prairie.

This house was not winterized and it only had running water as long as camp water was turned on. It had a small washroom and was only to be used until better facilities became available. When the water was turned off, all water had to be carried from the pump house. In the winter, melted snow was used for cleaning and sanitation. They had much snow that winter and didn't run out of water. The house also had a chimney and a heating stove.

The first winter was very trying. The chimney had deteriorated and it caught fire. Fortunately, it happened in the daytime just as my parents were sitting in the living room, and they saw it right away. God helped them to extinguish the blaze with the little water they had on hand and with the snow outside. However, they could not rekindle the fire in the stove and they had to live in their coats night and day until my father had rebuilt the chimney. With his knowledge as a brick mason, my father was able to do so without expensive cost.

After that cold winter, my parents moved into another house. The second house on the right side as you entered the camp. It is presently used as the "guest speakers'" cottage.

This house had one large room and three smaller ones, a front porch, a small hallway, and a toilet without a bath. My father was then granted permission to renovate the house as he saw fit. He converted the large room into a kitchen and dining area. He built cupboards and it became a cozy comfortable eating-place.

The room that contained the toilet was large enough to include a bathtub. He bought a good second-hand one and installed that. My husband had knowledge of plumbing and helped him.

A CONTINUOUS MIRACLE

He then dug a partial basement by hand—just high enough for him to stand upright, and wide enough to place a furnace and a workbench. It had an outside entrance as well as a drop staircase from the hallway upstairs. At that workbench he made the window shades for the cottages, and when keys were lost he made new ones. This workbench became his workshop during the long winter months.

Since Monday was my husband's and my day off at church, we would often go over to Big Prairie after the Sunday evening service and stay overnight and part of the next day. Alfred would give Dad a helping hand when needed. They purchased a studio coach, which opened into a bed for our use. This visit always brightened my parents' day and it also refreshed us from the week's stress.

It was at this time that the District contacted a well digger to dig for water so that my parents would have water all year around. Digging was charged by the foot, so when they reached 150 feet and found no water, my father became concerned about the price and stopped the digging, telling them not to return until they heard from him.

Dad then went into his bedroom and said to my mother, "Johanna, do not disturb me. I'm going to prayer and ask God for water." After some time he came out smiling and said, "I know where the water is." He went for a shovel and began digging. When he reached ten feet he struck water—plenty of water, good water. They never ran out, even during dry spells. He then called the digging company to come and get their rig. He did not need them any longer.

Nineteen fifty-two was the turning point in another milestone of my parents' lives. There were only a few cottages available for camp visitors, but there was a large barn that was converted into a women and men's dormitory.

Each person was given a cot and a straw tick for a mattress. It was my mother's duty to empty these ticks — or casings — each year, wash them, mend them if needed, and refill them again at the beginning of each new camp year. I assisted her in this work when we came to visit.

Lines were strung across the barn and these became the clothes racks and served as walls between the beds. Despite the disadvantages of our present day comforts, the Glory fell, God's people shouted, and discomforts were forgotten and even became fun.

The services were conducted in the area, which is now our dining room and the kitchen, and the dining area was below where the young people now congregate. Improvements were made yearly. The barn came down and was replaced with the hotel and the snack bar. The straw ticks were replaced with mattresses. New cement block dorms were also built. Although my father was the supervisor of the work and did much of it himself, there were willing ministers who came with members of their congregations on appointed days who helped with this work.

Outside families, with that I mean people who did not belong to our church fellowship, owned and lived in some of the houses around the lake. As they sold these homes, the camp bought them out, and year-by-year the camp became more private.

In those early years of camp, there was more responsibility placed upon the caretaker's wife. She had to do most of the work to get the camp ready. Washing all of the dishes, pots, and pans for another year of service was quite a chore. There was only one work day for the WMC'S to come and assist. D-con was placed on all of the mattresses in each cottage to keep the pest population under control. So on this WMC workday, all mattresses were placed outside to air. All rooms got a thorough cleaning. Clean curtains were hung, doilies were placed on dressers, and when everything was ready, it looked very inviting.

One year on this workday, clouds gathered, and a rainstorm threatened. All mattresses were outside and there wasn't enough help to get them back into the rooms in time. My mother then looked up into the sky, and as Elijah of old, demanded the clouds to dissipate. When they were finally finished, then the rain fell. She was then nicknamed Mrs. Elijah.

Kitchen work, at that time, was also more difficult. There were no fast foods, no instant potatoes, and no salad bars. Everything was made from scratch. Each year, a cook, one of our own people, was hired to do the cooking. Mother would make her way into the kitchen, often as early as 5:30. She would then peel potatoes, assist with cleaning the vegetables, and do wherever else was needed. The days were long and often she would return completely exhausted. She too, was in her seventies, and felt her age. However, she was faithful. It was God's business and she would do her best.

During the periods between camps, various ministers would drop by to help with painting or necessary repair work. Since, at that time, there was no "Essenhaus" in Shreve and no eating-place available in Big Prairie, Mother would prepare food to quench the hunger of these willing volunteers. Since she never knew when they would come, she had to be a minuteman, always ready.

I would like to say something about my father. He came into Pentecost from the Baptist church in 1914, but in 1918 he had a sad setback. He saw the inconsistency of a lady minister who had the gift of healing. Father could not understand how a woman could be used that mightily when she did not live up to God's requirements. He said to my mother, "If that is Pentecost, I don't want any of it." He never sought the Baptism of the Holy Spirit, although he loved the Lord deeply. Then, one day at camp, the Lord got hold of him. He was slain in the Spirit, and before God was through with him, he was speaking in a heavenly language. My mother was beside herself. She said, "Look, that starchy militant man lying there flat on his back. Praise God. He can do what no one else can."

From that day on, Dad was a changed man. He carried tracts in his pocket and left them with his testimony wherever he went. Even after his death, we heard statements from area businessmen who said, "He was a godly man." It was worth coming to Big Prairie, if for no other reason than that.

My mother was a woman of faith. I would like to tell you of some of her experiences while at camp.

She had lived most of her life in New Jersey and was not familiar with tornadoes. She was acquainted with hurricanes but not cyclones. One day while she was standing with my father outside of their house, a storm blew up. The sky was black and threatening. She saw a funnel cloud approaching the camp. She said to my father, "Look, William, I don't know what that is, but it isn't anything good." Lifting her hand in its direction she said, "You don't belong here. This is God's property. I rebuke you in the name of Jesus." Instantly the cloud turned directions and went toward Wooster where it did heavy damage, killing a clerk at the bank there.

No doubt you will remember the plastic fence around the swimming pool. One autumn day Dad was burning up the leaves around the pool. Believing that the fence was fiberglass, he allowed the flames to come up to the fence. To his surprise the fence caught fire. He wasn't prepared for that. He knew that the long house was in danger, so he grabbed the fence pole near the long house and pulled it out of the ground, thus breaking the circle of fire. Then he ran to the other extreme side to do the same, but his strength failed and instead of pulling out the pole, he fell in a dead faint right in the path of the flames.

Just then, Mother was prompted by the Holy Spirit to look out of the window. As she did, she saw huge columns of black smoke surrounding the pool. She ran outside calling "William, William," but got no answer.

Then, looking for him, she stumbled over his limp body. I asked her later, "What did you do?"

She replied with a question. "What do you suppose I did? I rebuked the faint in Jesus' name. He moved and I grabbed his hand, and with his assistance, I pulled him away just before the flames got to him." The neighbors called the fire department, but the flames were out before they got there. Isn't God faithful? Had Mother not listened to the promptings of the Spirit, the situation might not have turned out so victoriously.

My parents celebrated their Fiftieth wedding anniversary on May 7, 1957. The dining room was decorated with an arch filled with flowers and several large golden bells. It was a gala affair. Relatives came as far as from Germany. My father's oldest brother Karl and his wife, who were part of the original bridal party in Germany, were present. A quartet from Mansfield First Assembly, then known as Glad Tidings Tabernacle provided the music. The celebration lasted several days — one day at the church on Glessner Avenue and the other day at Big Prairie. On that day they celebrated at Big Prairie, my father took all the guests out to eat at San-Dar Restaurant in Belleville. It was the highlight of their life at Big Prairie.

Hildegarde Dehmel Jensen

Antique Lawn Mower

My parents were very faithful. They got up at 7 AM, even in the winter. In the summertime, when the duties at camp were more demanding, they would rise earlier. After their breakfast, they would have devotions, which they never missed. Then Dad would go to work sharpening the mower, checking the cottages, replacing broken glass where needed, and doing any number of items too numerous to mention. He checked the trees for dead limbs and made sure that they were cut down. Although cement work was heavy work, he laid the cement sidewalks from the dining room to the tabernacle. We still appreciate these to this day. He had to be about his Master's business. He said, "I'm getting paid and I must not waste the Lord's time."

In time they had to enlarge the eating-place downstairs. Some heavy two-by-six-inch beams that held up the upper sanctuary had to be replaced. One day, as we stopped to see my parents, we found my father lifting these immense beams all by himself. How he did it I'll never know, but he said the Lord showed him a way to do it.

However, he overtaxed his strength and weakened his heart. He was almost eighty years old when he plastered the walk-in. The Board of Health demanded that the walk-in be re-plastered or the camp would not be able to reopen for that season. Dad said, "Why pay out big money when I can do it?" So, that is what he did. But, instead of asking for someone to help him mix mortar and tend to him while he was up on the ladder, he did it himself. He had to go up and down the ladder every time he needed a fresh refill of mortar. When he had half of the ceiling done, his strength gave way. But, he couldn't stop or else there would have been a visible offset line on the ceiling and the Board of Health might have rejected the walk-in—they were hard on us Christians anyway. So Dad forced himself to finish it.

Consequently, at his age, he wore out his heart, which afterwards caused his death. I would often see him sitting in his truck trying to get some rest. If he went into the house to lie down Mother would say, "This is no time to rest—you can do that at night." She did not realize his weakened condition and she unknowingly made it more difficult for him. Therefore, he would rest in the truck so she couldn't see him.

One day when I found him sitting in his truck, he confided in me and said, "I almost died last night. I couldn't breathe." I encouraged him to see a doctor, which he did. Upon examination, the doctor said, "You have a worn-out heart and it can't be replaced. I would suggest that you be admitted to a hospital to see if they can help you some." Dad reluctantly consented.

I remember the day that we took him to the hospital. He pointed out a number of trees that had white markings on them. He said to me, "Tomorrow they are coming to cut down these trees with these white markings because they are dead. Will you check that it is done correctly?"

He then handed over a bunch of keys and carefully instructed me as to what each key covered. He then said, "Goodbye, my work is done."

Five days later on April 27, 1965, after 15 years of service, the Lord called him home. 2 Timothy 4:7-8 fits him well: "I have fought a good fight, I have finished my course and kept the faith. Henceforth there is laid up a crown of righteousness which the Lord, the righteous judge, shall give me at that day not to me only but unto all them that love his appearing."

Before closing, I would like to remark that my parents loved their stay at Big Prairie. I heard them say, "This has been the best 15 years of our lives." My father was so happy when the Tabernacle went up. He gave a helping hand when it was started but he never saw it completed. But I am sure that he is looking down from Glory and rejoicing over the progress that has been made at the camp.

Short Sermon

EVERY MORNING FRESH

Stephanie came home from school. As she entered the room she asked, "Grandma, do you have anything to eat? I'm starved." She hurried into the kitchen, opened the cupboard, and grabbed a box of her favorite cereal. She poured it into a dish, got out the milk, and eagerly took a spoon full of it. Her nose curled and pushing the dish aside she exclaimed, "It's stale. Don't you have something better?"

Who likes stale food? Even God doesn't.

God instructed Israel to gather manna "EVERY MORNING FRESH". He turned the bitter waters of Marah sweet and He gave them clear, clean water out of the rock. He wanted His children to have the best.

Water is so important. Without it no one can live. The body needs it. Vegetation needs it.

In Formosa they spent $22 million to dig 1750 water wells for their rice production. This increased their output by almost 300 thousand tons yearly. Just think what it would be like to get up and find no water.

Many years ago, during an interim period, we moved into an unfinished house in the fall of the year. When we awoke in the morning we discovered that all water pipes had frozen. Had it not been for a kind neighbor who offered us bathroom facilities and gave our family breakfast, no doubt our children would have missed school that day. Yes, water is so important in more than one way.

1. A Fresh Cleansing

How can you clean anything without water?

Most people, when they arise in the mornings, take a shower. Why? Because it refreshes, it cleanses, and gives a good start for the day. They are not like the old lady who lived in the Kentucky Mountains and who had not had a bath in years. She was so crusted that it took five tubs of water to get her clean.

Throughout the Bible, God is always asking us to be clean. The prophets Isaiah and Ezekiel continually asked Israel to put away the evil of their doings. Even the priests in the Old Testament, before entering the office of their priestly duties, went through a purifying process. Every time they approached the altar of sacrifice they had to stop at the laver and wash their hands and feet, before they could go into the tabernacle to worship.

Why was it so important? Because they daily rubbed elbows with people who were unclean. That touch often contaminated them too.

Likewise, we also, as we mingle with an ungodly people need to be cleansed from the touch of contamination, as well as our own shortcomings.

"Let us draw near with a true heart in full assurance of faith, having our hearts sprinkled from an evil conscience and our bodies washed with pure water." Hebrews 10:22

Robert Lawry so amply penned the words to the song:

What can wash away my sins?
Nothing but the blood of Jesus.
Go to Calvary's stream, take a dip, and come up clean.

2. A Fresh Drink

The water of this world cannot quench the thirsting soul. A good example is the Samaritan woman at the well. In the conversation that Jesus had with her He said to her, "But whosoever drinketh of the water that I shall give him shall never thirst; but the water that I shall give him shall be in him a well of water springing up into everlasting life." John 4:14

The woman said to him, "Sir, give me this water, that I thirst not."

This water of eternal life, that Jesus gives, quenches all the desires for the water of this world. If you still thirst for earthly things then you haven't tasted of the water that Jesus wants to give you. A fresh drink is so important.

After graduating Bible College, my husband's first charge was a small country church in Athens, Wisconsin. We moved into a house that had no running water.

Water had to be carried from a well. In order to make it more convenient for me, Alfred, my husband, dug a ditch and laid pipe from the well to the house, thus bringing the water into the kitchen. He then installed a pitcher pump that we primed. It saved me many steps and energy.

One day we all got sick. I checked my icebox, but there was no problem. Then Alfred said, "I'm going to check the well." He returned smiling and said, "I found the cause. A mole fell into the well. It drowned, decayed, and polluted the water."

Then came the cleanup. Alfred placed a ladder into the well, and with a broom, he scrubbed the sides thoroughly. Then with a pump, he pumped the well dry. This he did three times. After that we were no longer sick.

Spiritually speaking, do you have some moles in your water? Moles like a spirit of hatred or unforgiveness, a spirit of pride and selfishness, or gossip and mud flinging? Do you have sexual habits or unfaithfulness? These things will make you sick and you will lose the joy of your salvation. Begin scrubbing and clean out the well.

3. Fresh Manna

The Israelites, walking through the wilderness, became very hungry. "What shall we eat?" They partitioned Moses. They began to murmur and Moses spoke to the Lord about it.

God then appeared in a cloud of glory and said, "I have heard the murmurings of the Children of Israel, and at evening they shall eat flesh, and in the morning they shall be filled with bread: and they shall know that I am the Lord their God."

According to Exodus 16:14: "And when the dew disappeared later in the morning it left tiny flakes of something as small as hoarfrost on the ground" (LB translation).

And when they saw it, they said one to another, "It is manna." They were commanded to gather it "EVERY MORNING FRESH." They were not to leave any for the next day. Notwithstanding they hearkened not unto Moses; but some of them left of it until the morning, and it bred worms, and stank. There was one exception and that was on the Sabbath. Then they could gather for two days.

There is a lesson in this for the Church today. We cannot live on yesterday's experience, or yesterday's bread. We need FRESH BREAD EVERYDAY. Jesus said in St. John 6:35, "I am the bread of life: he that cometh to me shall never hunger; and he that believeth on me shall never thirst."

St. John 1:1 states, "In the beginning was the Word (Jesus), and the Word (Jesus) was with God, and the Word (Jesus) was God."

The Word—the Scriptures, Jesus—is our bread and we must consume it daily. It must come alive and be FRESH in our lives every day. If our Christian experience gets stale then our testimony will stink and we will never win the world for Christ.

4. A Fresh Anointing

Have you ever felt an inward urge to pray—a pulling at your heartstrings? Jesus so much wants to bless us but He can't because we are not available.

I'll never forget the morning in Bridgman, Michigan, when I felt this strong urge to pray. I felt the Spirit urging me, but I wanted to get my housework done first. So I bargained with the Lord. I procrastinated. In my time, I would do so. But I learned a lesson I will never forget. It doesn't pay to disobey.

We were living in an apartment above the church which Alfred, my husband, had built. Our bathroom was adjacent to the living room above the rest room downstairs. We had a set of twins, Danny and Dolly, who had watched my husband as he worked on the plumbing.

Just when I thought I was through with my work, and I was

Twins Daniel and Dolores Jensen

ready to pray, these twins got an idea. Dolly said to Danny, "I saw Father hook this sink up to the wall, wonder if we could lift it off." So they tried. Dolly was on one side and Danny on the other. Surprisingly enough, they succeeded. They pulled the pipe apart and the water gushed out. The commotion and the noise brought me running. What had they done? They were both sitting in the bathtub to keep dry, but my work was just beginning.

Alfred had previously showed me where the water turnoff valve was in the basement. I ran down but could not find it. My parents lived in the house next to us, but both my father and my husband were not at home. I ran to the plumber, two houses away, but he too was not at home. All this time the water was running.

My conscience began to condemn me. I could hear the Lord saying, "Had you prayed when I called you, all this would not have happened."

I was guilty. I cried out to the Lord, "Please forgive me and show me where the shutoff valve is." I ran back into the basement, and there in front of me, was the valve. It was there all the time, but in my excitement I overlooked it. I turned it off but then the cleaning process began. If it had not been for my mother, I don't know what I would have done. Not only did our apartment need attention, but the church downstairs needed cleaning as well. Water was everywhere.

When it was all over I fell on my knees and wept like a baby. The Lord was merciful and I again felt His peace and forgiveness. I could say with David in Psalm 133:2, "It is like the precious ointment upon the head, that ran down upon the beard, even Aaron's beard: that went down to the skirts of his garments." I felt the anointing oil all over me.

How about you? Are you hungry for a fresh piece of that heavenly manna? For a drink of that clear sparkling water and for the anointing that will soak you good? God has it for you. Go get it . . .

Poetry

AUTUMN

The golden-red is yellow
The corn is turning brown.
The trees in Apple Orchards
With fruit are bending down.

The asters by the brook side
Are swaying in the breeze
While birds silhouette the skies
Flying south for greener trees.

Orange and red, yellow and brown
Are colors in the tree's crown,
As the master painter dips his brush
In bright colors with his touch.

Horse-drawn loads of fresh cut hay
Attract the youngsters in their play
Whistling merrily as they ride
Down the road, side by side.

Golden pumpkins with smiling faces
Line the walks at various places.

A CONTINUOUS MIRACLE

Children everywhere are having fun
Frolicking in the autumn sun.

Hildegard Dehmel Jensen

LIVING LIFE

The greatest skill in all the earth,
Is to grow old with laughter and mirth.
To rest, when you'd like to work
Keep silent when being irked
To suffer pain without complaint
And remain strong and never faint.

Hildegard Dehmel Jensen

THE POSTAGE STAMP

There was a little postage stamp
No bigger than your thumb
But it stuck right to the job
Until its work was done.
They licked and pounded it
Till it would make you sick
And the more it took a licking
The better it would stick.

Let's all be like the postage stamp
In play, in life's rough game
And just keep on a-sticking
Though we hang our heads in shame.
The stamp stuck to the letter
Till it saw it safely through

Hildegarde Dehmel Jensen

There's no one doing better
Let's keep sticking and be true.

Hildegard Dehmel Jensen

BETHEL

One by one we entered those doors
And walked on hallowed ground over those
   floors
Our hearts were touched by the flame of God's
   love
As it filled our hearts from God above
We ate and drank from a heavenly source
Moved about through the power of that God
   given force.

The truths that we learned were never forgotten
Because they were of God begotten.
Our teachers were full of knowledge, wisdom,
   and power
And they became to us a mighty tower.
Our faith grew amidst tests and trials
As we courageously conquered Satan's wiles.

Our paths were divided as God led the way
Leaning firm on His arm we followed day by
   day.
Some remained East and some went West
Knowing God's leadings were always the best.
Some were led South, for there too was a flock
That needed to be built on that solid rock.

Those who went over-seas to build God's work

A CONTINUOUS MIRACLE

No sacrifice, difficulties, nor dangers did they shirk.
God gave them miracles and met their needs
As they continued to plant the sacred seed.
Did God forsake? Oh no! He did not.
Neither did they doubt God nor their lot.

Today, as we reminisce the paths we've trod
We give thanks to our wonderful God.
There were days of conquest, victory, and joy
As well as defeat when efforts lay trampled as a twisted toy.
Our hope and our faith look forward to the day
When He, Himself, will give us our eternal pay.

Hildegard Dehmel Jensen

A SPECIAL MOTHER

A Mother's someone special
With an understanding heart.
When others lose their faith in you
That's just when hers will start.

A Mother's someone loving
Who has the sweetest way
Of giving you encouragement
When skies are looking gray.

Hildegarde Dehmel Jensen

A Mother's someone loving
Who will always lend a hand
And smooth things out a little
When they don't go as planned.

A Mother's someone dearly loved
And that is surely true
Of a mother who is all these things
A Mother just like you.

Thank you, Mother, for you are very special
For showing love, concern, and care
I'll always appreciate the tidbits
That you so graciously shared.

Hildegard Dehmel Jensen

DAN

Remember my Son, God's work for you is never done.
Until bowing before Him — when earth's race is won
As the holy oil was placed on Aaron's brow
So the anointing covered you — never forget that vow.
At the altar, at camp, God gave you His call
From it you never dare fall.

Today, your heart may be heavy and yet it can be bright
As your path changes directions in this spiritual life.
Remember! The days you worked in the school of hard knocks

A CONTINUOUS MIRACLE

Twins Daniel and Dolores Jensen

When people's hearts and heads were often as
　　hard as rocks.
But GOD took you through, and will continue to
　　do so
Just keep trusting Him as onward you go.

The fields are many, the harvest is great
The Lord will lead you through another gate.
Never get weary, distressed, or give up
For within your hand you hold Salvation's cup.
Satan can never stop you — it lies in your power
To defeat him at every turn and every hour.

Hildegarde Dehmel Jensen

Lift up your heads, precious children, courageously press on
And constantly hold the powerful prayer wand.
Prayer is the weapon of victory, without it you'll fail
But with it you can face every gale.
Fight the good fight of FAITH until life's work is done,
And then the crown of life, with rewards, will be won.

Hilde Dehmel Jensen

STEPHANIE

You are so very precious
So innocent and small
Soon to be bubbling with excitement
At the wonder of it all.

You watch with bright and trusting eyes
Dancing from place to place
And when you smile, the world will see the joy that
Shines from such a little face!

Wouldn't it be wonderful
To save the things you see
That sweet and tender love of life
That baby ecstasy?

Wouldn't you love to bottle it
And keep it tucked away
The ultimate gift of happiness
Just in case you run out someday?

A CONTINUOUS MIRACLE

We wish you truth and tenderness
To last your lifetime through
So all your wonderful childlike faith
Can shine in everything you do.

May Jesus touch your little life
And always help for you to see
Things to help to make you be
Everything He intended for you to be.

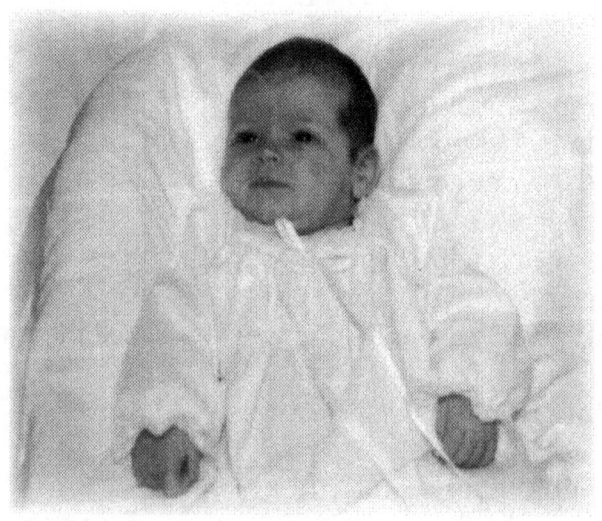

Stephanie

Hildegarde Dehmel Jensen

MORTGAGE BURNING

FIRST ASSEMBLY OF GOD
Mansfield, Ohio
June 17, 1990

With Thomas Ken we now can sit
As our final debt we now have paid
"Praise God from whom all blessings flow
Praise Him, all creatures here below
Praise Him above, ye heavenly host
Praise Father, Son and Holy Ghost."

Twenty-one years ago we rejoiced,
For it was then
The kindhearted banker money did lend
Enabling us God's house to build
With joy and praise
Our hearts were filled
Today, again, we bless the Lord
And praise His name in one accord.

As the mortgage burns in flames of fire
May our spirits be lifted even higher
Let us press on with hearts
Filled with love
For Brothers and Sisters and God above
Let us unflinchingly run the race
Until we see our Savior's face.

Rev. Hildegard Jensen

A CONTINUOUS MIRACLE

SILVER BELLS

I took a man — so handsome and tall,
He was single, a farmer, and really could throw
    a basketball
"Who is this guy", said Dolly, standing by
For I am out to make him mine.
A courtship developed — Wedding Bells ran
And a fruitful, happy life began.

Today, as the Silver Wedding Bells ring
We've joined to help them ring.
Days were not always sunny — there were some
    clouds
There were those painful, hurtful rounds
But God's given faith helped them to stand
As they held to God's unchanging hand.

God blessed them with three wonderful girls
To them they are more precious than pearls.
God's blessings have not yet ceased
Upon them, more will yet be released.
The secret of life rests with the Lord
For, in Him, there is a great reward.

Written for Frank & Dolly Giauque's Twenty-Fifth Wedding Anniversary
By Hildegard Dehmel Jensen

Hildegarde Dehmel Jensen
DEATH TURNED TO VICTORY

Beyond the clouds there is a bright tomorrow
For those who have met the Lord — there is no
   sorrow.
For Christ removed the sting of death and sin
Prepared the way for us a new life to begin.

Our carnal human eyes are often so blinded,
With pleasure and wealth so worldly minded
That spiritual values are hid from view
And those that find them are rare and few.

But there is a hope — it's within our reach
An endless joy, the Word of God does teach
To find this life you must believe,
And Christ Jesus into your heart receive.

Then death is turned to Victory
As this present life becomes history.
And before our eyes a new life unfolds
More glorious than ever could be told.

Karen is now enjoying this glorious life
Free from anxiety, worry, and strife
She will be missed in the house of the Lord
But will be receiving her heavenly reward.

Hilde Dehmel Jensen

A CONTINUOUS MIRACLE

ELWOOD

*Written by Hilde Jensen
(Elwood's mother-in law)
for Elwood's Homegoing
October 16, 1991*

Elwood

When the trials of life are over
And our work on earth is done
There is a brighter tomorrow
After the setting of the sun.

Only "Glory By and By"
Is a song we joyfully sing
And today Elwood joins the saints
Making the gates of Heaven ring.

Singing was his fondest joy
Singing with his brothers when he was a boy
From early morn till late at night
He praised his Lord with all his might.

If he could speak to you today
I know you would hear him say
It's not a tale or fiction too
This life is real and very true.

To enter in you must come to the Lord
To miss this step you can't afford.
I can hear Elwood calling you
Come, Jesus loves you too.

H.D. Jensen

Hildegarde Dehmel Jensen

MOTHER

May the God of Comfort give to you
Strength and courage to carry you through,
The Valley of Sorrow is not easy to cross
For the death of a Mother is a great loss.

But Jesus extends his hand to you
To give to you a much clearer view
Of the glories of heaven she now shares
No longer earth's sorrows to bear

So look up my child, strength comes from above,
The Lord will fill your heart with heavens' love.
And soon, we all will share the blessing
Of Eternal Joy in which she is now resting.

Hilde Dehmel Jensen

FORGIVEN

Forgiven, child of mine, you are forgiven
Don't question my love when it is given.
I know all, I see your heart
It lies before me as an open chart.

I've washed it clean, I've removed each spot.
Believe, accept — I lie not.

It's not your doing that can change a thing
It's the power that can make your heart sing.
Begin right now — let your praises ring
You'll find your heart free from everything.

I love you so, you are my son

For you I've died — the victory is won.
The power of Satan is broken forever
My love and presence will leave you never.

So go in peace, rejoice in me
Only glory is ahead you see.
Rejoice and sing, lift your heart to me
A chosen vessel for me now you'll be.

Hildegard Dehmel Jensen
This poem is given by the Lord — Aug. 8, 1981

DEDICATION FOR FIRST ASSEMBLY OF GOD
Mansfield, Ohio — February 13, 1970

Small was the beginning, as in houses they met
Forward they went with a faith that was set.
Stronger they grew and larger, too,
Until they moved into something brand new.

'Twas just a basement, but what a thrill
As the large auditorium with believers was filled.
Then came a storm which tore them apart,
And pierced the saints like a sharp dart.

Through rain and sunshine, and all kinds of weather
Though sharp blew the storm — it was always for better.
Faith was increased as God led the way,
To a path that ended in a brighter day.

Glad Tidings Tabernacle, 1938. James Wilkerson, pastor.

Glad Tidings Tabernacle Assembly of God, 1950. Built by pastor, Alfred Jensen

A CONTINUOUS MIRACLE

Leaders came and leaders went
Leading them on and mending the rent.
It was a bright day when the walls went up
Though rain trickled through, it was caught in a cup.
The greater the trial, the harder they worked.
God's task in no way they shirked.
Then one Sunday morning a lady fair,
Came forward and contributed her share.

A thousand dollars—in a lump sum.
Oh! What rejoicing and what fun.
The following day a bill was due,
And for God to provide was nothing new.

And so they went from that day to this
No good thing God's people would miss.
Again the building was small,
As on God's name they daily called.

First Assembly of God. Clinton Vanzant, pastor.

Hildegarde Dehmel Jensen

Their name was changed like Abram of old,
And many new sheep were brought into the fold.
A new horizon before them arose,
Forward they went, though some did oppose.

Today upon new ground they set their feet,
As in this new temple from now on they'll meet.
May God bless their efforts as forward they go;
Determined to conquer—no fear to show.

Tonight, we dedicate this church to Him.
Praises ever to the highest we'll bring.
To new horizons and brighter days
Ever be led in glorious ways.

Mrs. H.E. Jensen
(Former pastor's wife)

Mansfield, Glad Tidings Tabernacle Assembly of God name changed to Mansfield First Assembly of God

About The Author

HILDEGARDE E. DEHMEL JENSEN
September 9. 1909–October 2, 1996

Rev. Hildegard E. Dehmel Jensen was an ordained minister with the Assemblies of God Fellowship. She attended Bethel Bible College in New Jersey, which later became Central Bible College in Springfield, Missouri. She pioneered and pastored many churches with her husband Alfred J. Jensen—in Oklahoma, Nebraska, Wisconsin, Michigan, and Ohio. The first churches were all German speaking, affiliated with the German Branch from Cleveland, Ohio, later transferring to all English-speaking churches. She stayed active all her life in the Lord's ministry, teaching, preaching, visiting, serving as hospital Chaplain, working with Aglow ministry, and being a help to where ever she was needed. She also was a skilled secretary and typist. She had an interest in writing and poetry.

She had three children, the oldest, Ruth Louise Jensen Orewiler, and a set of twins that were always the joy of the family, Delores Johanna Jensen Davies Giauque and Rev. Daniel William Jensen. The twins were known as Danny and Dolly.

The following article was published June 23, 1988 in the Tribune-Courier, *Ontario, Ohio, and is reprinted with permission.*

WOMAN RENEWS LICENSE EVERY YEAR: HAS BEEN MINISTER 44 YEARS

By Helen C. Graham

For almost 44 years, Hildegard E. Jensen, mother of Mrs. Elwood E. (Ruth) Orewiler, Rock Rd., Ontario, has been an ordained minister with the Assembly of God Church, a position that was almost unheard of for a woman in October of 1944, when she was ordained at the Immanuel Assembly of God Church in Cleveland, a German branch church, during a church conference.

Rev. Mrs. Jensen renews her license each year and continues to serve the Mansfield area in various ways.

She said, "I was called to God before I was born."

She explained the calling. "My mother, Johanna Dehmel, age 26 after three years of marriage, prayed for a child, promising to return the child to God's service. She compared her situation to Hannah in the Bible, who prayed for a child and had Samuel."

Hildegard was born in Muelheim, Germany, Sept. 16, 1909, the only child of William H. and Johanna Dehmel.

Influenced by his brother Karl, who had come to the United States the year before, William Dehmel worked as a machinist and singer to earn enough money for their fare and the family came to Elizabeth, New Jersey, in May of 1914.

Another native of Germany, Alfred John Jensen, came to New Jersey when he was 21.

An acquaintance who worked for a steamship line asked Mr. Dehmel, a mason and contractor, I he had any work for the young immigrant, Alfred Jensen. Hildegard was the book-keeper and office manager for her father; so he gave Alfred his first job and then met him in the German-speaking church her family attended in Elizabeth.

Romance blossomed between Hildegard and Alfred. They were married Dec. 30, 1933, in her family home.

He enrolled for three years at Southwestern Bible College, formerly of Enid, Oklahoma, now in Waxahachie, Texas, and was graduated in 1935. He was ordained in October, 1936, at the Immanuel Assembly of God Church in Cleveland.

She went to Bethel College in Newark, New Jersey, now in Springfield, Missouri, and renamed Central Bible College. When she was graduated in three years, she was told, "The church does not ordain ladies."

While attending college at Enid, Jensen was a student pastor at a local church. The Jensens' first child, Ruth, was born in Enid.

A CONTINUOUS MIRACLE

The Rev. Mr. Jensen's first church was in Athens, Wisconsin, at $15 a week. One parishioner criticized Hildegard for buying a rug for $25.

In August of 1987, Mr. And Mrs. Arthur Diedrich, who had been members of the Athens, Wisconsin, church 50 years ago, came to visit Rev. Mrs. Jensen in Mansfield. There were many memories recounted then, she said.

Their next church was in Scotts Bluff, Nebraska, where their twin son and daughter were born.

Rev. Mr. Jensen was a builder. At every church throughout his ministry, he added something to the church. At Athens, Wisconsin, he put a prayer room in the church basement and soundproofed it. At Scotts Bluff, he drew up plans himself and built a parsonage for the church.

They next went to Bridgman, Michigan, 20 miles west of Benton Harbor. He built a parsonage there with three bedrooms, large living room, dining room, kitchen and bath, which they occupied for the eight years they were there.

She said, "The small congregation has decided my husband was the last pastor they would try. It was a small group of people having problems among themselves. We must have helped them because today that church has a 10-acre campground and a retirement center and is planning to build a larger church."

From Bridgman they came to Immanuel Church on Wayne St. in Mansfield, a post he held for 10 years. During this time, she was ordained and they served as co-pastors there and with a church in Akron, alternating Sundays. While there, Rev. Mr. Jensen took down one whole wall and took off an outside chimney of the parsonage and built a kitchen, large living room and dining room.

While at Immanuel Church, Rev. Mrs. Jensen worked at Hoff Manufacturing Company on North Diamond St., where she was a secretary and payroll clerk. When it was her turn to preach at the Akron Church, she walked to the train depot and sat in the depot in Akron until somebody picked her up and took her to the church.

When she took the train back to Mansfield, she walked from the depot at 2 am to her house on Wayne St.; then got up to go to work on Monday morning. When it was her husband's turn to preach in Akron and hers to preach in Immanuel, he drove the car there.

They left Immanuel church in 1950 and went to Glad Tidings Tabernacle on Glessner Ave., Mansfield, where the congregation was meeting in a basement. Rev. Mr. Jensen constructed the church building over the basement. They stayed there eight years and went to Martins Ferry, Ohio, where he described the meeting place as a disgrace.

When they arrived at Martins Ferry, they found the congregation meeting in a small brick building that was a men's washroom for area coal miners. When the mine closed, the congregation rented the washroom. Rev. Mr. Jensen built Trinity Assembly of God Church, a stone structure a block long in the heart of the city.

That church today has grown so much that the congregation is looking for larger facilities. After about 10 years there, they went to Oberlin, Ohio, where they built the Maranatha Temple. Rev. Mr. Jensen retired at age 72 from the Oberlin church.

While they were there, Rev. Mrs. Jensen performed four marriages by request; her husband would not marry divorced persons.

How did the various congregations react to one of the first woman ministers?

"Only one place did I find negative feelings," she said, "and the people did adjust." She did not identify that church.

During the years they were co-pastors in Akron and Mansfield, she preached in English and German. "Whenever my husband was not available," she said. "I never took it from him. I did not believe in usurping a man's position; but whenever he needed me, I preached."

In later years, they left the German branch of the Assembly of God denomination and remained with the English branch.

Rev. Mr. Jensen never received any money for any of the building he did. He was never paid anything for it. "He gets his reward in heaven," she said, adding, "We worked together as best we could."

She went with her husband on a missionary trip to Jamaica for two weeks, during which she gave a training class for Sunday School teachers. She began teaching Sunday School at age 15 and has taught for more than 64 years. She has a Sunday School class now at the First Assembly of God Church on McPherson St.

Thru the years, she has sung in church choirs and has directed choirs.

All of her rewards are not waiting for her in heaven; some have come to her here. She is listed in *Who's Who in Women's Ministry for 1986-87* and she received the "Encourager of the Year Award" last Oct. 16 at Ashland College during a three-day convention of Flame International, a charismatic organization based in Dallas, Texas.

She is interested in writing, especially children's stories. Her book, *Battles for the Mind,* is in preparation.

Today Rev. Mrs. Jensen speaks to women's groups and had taken training as a volunteer with Richland

Pregnancy Services. She has a special phone at her home for scheduling counseling sessions for pregnant girls with professional counselors.

She has been a widow since August 1, 1983. Her family includes Ruth Orewiler of Ontario, a school teacher, Dolly, also a school teacher, who is married to Frank Giauque and living in Stillwell, Holmes County, Ohio; and Rev. Danny Jensen and his wife, Evelyn, of Splendora, Texas; nine grandchildren and four great-grandchildren.

Assembly of God — Bridgeman, Michigan. Left, Pastor and Mrs. A.J. Jensen. Front row center, twins Danny & Dolly Jensen, Rita Hartwig, and with long curls, Ruth Jensen.

www.ingramcontent.com/pod-product-compliance
Lightning Source LLC
Chambersburg PA
CBHW031248290426
44109CB00012B/492